Ceredigion

WALKS

Compiled by
Terry Marsh

D1611824

JARROLD

Text:	Terry Marsh
Photography:	Terry Marsh
Editorial:	Ark Creative (UK) Ltd
Design:	Ark Creative (UK) Ltd

Series Consultant: Brian Conduit

© Jarrold Publishing, an imprint of Pitkin Publishing Ltd

OS Ordnance Survey® This product includes mapping data licensed from Ordnance Survey® with the permission of the Controller of Her Majesty's Stationery Office. © Crown Copyright 2008. All rights reserved. Licence number 100017593. Ordnance Survey, the OS symbol and Pathfinder are registered trademarks and Explorer, Landranger and Outdoor Leisure are trademarks of the Ordnance Survey, the national mapping agency of Great Britain.

Jarrold Publishing   ISBN 978-0-7117-4993-1

First published 2003 by Jarrold Publishing
Revised and reprinted 2008

Printed in Singapore. 2/08

Pitkin Publishing Ltd
Healey House, Dene Road, Andover, Hampshire SP10 2AA
e-mail: info@totalwalking.co.uk
www.totalwalking.co.uk

Front cover: Plynlimon Fawr and Ynys Lochtyn (inset)
Previous page: Allt Wen and Cardigan Bay

Contents

Keymap — 4
At-a-glance... walks chart — 6
Introduction — 8
Walks

1 Pen Dinas — 12

2 Cwm Rheidol — 14

3 Teifi Marshes and the Afon Teifi — 16

4 Furnace and the Dyfi Estuary — 18

5 Cwmtydu — 20

6 Little Quay Bay and Afon Drywi — 22

7 Cardigan and St Dogmaels Abbey — 24

8 Llangranog and Ynys Lochtyn — 26

9 Llanbadarn Fawr — 29

10 Aber Teifi — 32

11 Aberaeron to Aberarth — 35

12 Aberaeron to Henfynyw — 38

13 Plynlimon — 41

14 Strata Florida — 44

15 Penbryn — 47

16 Devil's Bridge and the Mynach Valley — 50

17 Soar y Mynydd and the Afon Doethie — 53

18 Llanerchaeron — 56

19 Aberystwyth to Clarach Bay — 59

20 Trefechan to Morfa Bychan — 62

21 Trefeurig — 64

22 Tresaith and Aberporth — 67

23 Borth — 71

24 Llyn Brianne — 74

25 Pen y Garn — 77

26 Nant-y-moch — 80

27 New Quay — 83

28 Teifi Pools Walk — 87

Further Information — 90

The National Trust; The Ramblers' Association; Walkers and the Law; Glossary of Welsh Words; Countryside Access Charter; Global Positioning System (GPS); Safety on the Hills; Useful Organisations; Ordnance Survey Maps

Short, easy walks

Walks of modest length, likely to involve some modest uphill walking

More challenging walks which may be longer and/or over more rugged terrain, often with some stiff climbs

SCALE 1:277 777 or 1 INCH to about 4½ MILES *1CM to 2.7KM*

0 2 4 6 8 10 **KILOMETRES** 15

0 2 4 6 **MILES** 8 10

KEYMAP HEIGHTS SHOWN IN METRES

C A R D I G A N   B A

B A E   C E R E D I G

Cardigan Island

Gwbert Ferwig

Y Ferwig

Parclyn

Blaenannerch

10

7

St Dogmaels

Bridell

3

Monington

Pen-y-bryn

lanrhyd

Llantood

Rhos-Hill

592 789

B4332

Newchapel

Penrherber

B4332

**CARDIGAN/
ABERTEIFI**

Llangoedmor

Llechryd

Castle

Cilgerran

Abercych

Cenarth

Cwm Cou

**NEWCASTLE
EMLYN**

Treman

Penparc

577

Pantgwyn

Ponthirwaun

Bryngwyn

Capel Tygwydd

Pentrecagal

583

Blaenporth

Betws
Ifan

591

Brongest

Beulah

496

Tan-y-groes

Sarnau

Glynarthen

B4334

Rhydlewis

Troedyraur

Maesllyn

Llandyfriog

Aber
banc

Henllan

Croes-lan

Horeb

Penrhiw-llan

Aberporth

Tresaith

Penbryn

22

Brynhoffnant

787

Pentregat

Penrhiwpal

Capel
Cynon

Floesyrasol

Tregroes

Pren
gwyn

1031

Gwardalog

955

Moel y Mor

Pont-Sian

Rhydowen

Capel
Dewi

Llandysul

Llanfihangel-
ar-arth

Llangeler

1097

B433

Cwmtydu

5

Nanternis

Ynys-Lochtyn a

8

Llangranog

15

Plwmp

A487

Llwyndafydd

Pontgarreg

744

Synod Inn

A486

**NEW
QUAY**

27

Giflachreda

Cross
Inn

6

Foss-y-ffin

Llwyncelyn

Llangarreglwyd

A486

Llanarth

Oakford

Mydroilyn

Caledrhydiau

Talgarreg

Bwlch-y-fadfa

640

1020

Castell
Howell

B4337

846

B433

Aberar

ABERAERON

1

12

1

1062

TYWYN
Rhyd-yr-onen
Trum Gelli
Pennal
Cwrt
A493
Dovey
Penegoes
MACHYNLLETH
Corlan-fraith
Caethle
Forge
Afon Dulas
Derwenlas
Glaspwll
Pant-glas
Aberdyfi
914
AFON DYFI
4
Aberdovey Bar
RIVER DOVEY
Furnace
Cors Fochno
Pencarreg-gopa
1467
Cwm Einion
A487
1662
Ynyslas
B4353
Llancynfelyn
Tre'r-ddol
Tre Taliesin
1708
Moel-y-Llyn
Cwm Ceulan
New Pool
1909
Borth
Tal-y-bont
1837
Upper Borth
Dol-y-Bont
Cefnrhysgarth
Drosgol
1806
23
Llandre
A487
Afon Leri
Bont-goch or Elerch
26
2467
Drum Peithnant
13
Bow Street
Salem
Llyn Syfydrin
1435
1661
Llangorwen
21
PLYNLIMON
PUMLUMON
19
Penrhyn-coch
Plas Gogerddan
Pen-bont
Capel Dewi
Rhydypennau
Cwmerfyn
ABERYSTWYTH
Comins Coch
Llanbadarn Fawr
Ponterwyd
The Bar
Pen Dinas
A44
Capel Bangor
Cwmbrwyno
Goginan
B4343
Capel Seion
Ysbyty Cynfyn
1
2
1304
A4120
Aberffrwd
Ystumtuen
20
9
989
Gors
12
16
New Cross
Llanfihangel-y-Creuddyn
1045
2003
Afon Ystwyth
Bryn Garw
147
Cnwch Coch
25
Blaenplwyf
B4340
1274
Pentre-llyn
Llanilar
Cwmystwyth
Rhadmad
B4575
447
1085
Llanafan
Pont-rhyd-y-groes
Llanddeiniol
B4576
Mynydd Bach
Ysbyty Ystwyth
Carreg Ti-pw
Llangwyryfon
Lledrod
Trawsallt
Llanrhystud
18
Tynygraig
1092
1944
1721
Trefenter
A485
Ystradmeurig
A487
1183
Ffair-Rhos
Llan-non
Rhyd-Rosser
Ffosheiyg
Pontrhydfendigaid
28
Bronnant
Swyddffynnon
14
Strata Florida Abbey
1738
Nebo
Bontnewydd
Dibyn Du
Bethania
1129
Blaenpennal
Cross Inn
711
Pen-y-bwlch
Pennant
617
B4577
818
Monachty
B4337
Cors-goch Glan Teifi
Penuwch
B4576
761
Llangeitho
Tregaron
1799
Cilcennin
637
B4342
Y Drum
Bwlch-Llan
1668
Bryn Crwn
1732
Ty-nant
Capel Betws Lleucu
SARN HELEN
Trefilan
Llundain-fach
Abermeurig
Tal-sarn
Pont Llanio
Esgair Fraith
1592
Llyn Berwyn
Esgair Cerrig
Gamallt
Ystrad Aeron
Gartheli
Llwyn-y-groes
Llanddewi Brefi
1588
B4342
Felinfach
825
Esgair Llethr
Temple Bar
635
1543
1644
Cefn Coch
17
Betws Bledrws
Llangybi
1521
Pont Creuddyn
Llanfair Clydogau
Bryn Brawd
1589
Pen Rhiwclochdy
Pen'y Gurnos
Cefn Fanog
1476
Cribyn
1497
Llyn Brianne
Silian
Glan Denys
A482
A485
850
Craig Twrch
1445
Mynydd Trawsnant
Cwrtnewydd
LAMPETER
Cellan
1695
Penre-bach
Afon Twrch
24
Llanwnnen
Cwmann
Afon Teifi
1444
Ystradffin
A475
Dre-fach
Llanycrwys
Alltyblaca
1515
Ffarmers
Cwrt-y-cadno
Rhandirmwyn
Pencarreg
Ffaldybrenin
Mynydd Mallaen
Bryn Nicol
1360
Llanybydder
Mynydd Pencarreg
Esgair Ferchon
B4337
Llandre
Aber-Giar
Afon Tywi
Cilycwm
Pumsaint
Llanllwni
1339
1120
Cynghordy
Caio
762
Rhydcymerau

Walk	Page	Start	Nat. Grid Reference	Distance	Time	Highest Point
Aberaeron to Aberarth	35	Aberaeron	SN 456630	4¼ miles (6.8km)	2 hrs	443ft (135m)
Aberaeron to Henfynyw	38	Aberaeron	SN 456630	4½ miles (7.2km)	2 hrs	413ft (126m)
Aberystwyth to Clarach Bay	59	Aberystwyth	SN 581818	6¼ miles (10km)	3 hrs	475ft (145m)
Aber Teifi	32	Cardigan	SN 156460	4¼ miles (6.8km)	2 hrs	100ft (30m)
Borth	71	Borth	SN 608890	6½ miles (10.5km)	3 hrs	328ft (100m)
Cardigan and St Dogmaels Abbey	24	Cardigan	SN 156460	4 miles (6.4km)	2 hrs	367ft (112m)
Cwm Rheidol	14	Cwm Rheidol Reservoir Visitor Centre	SN 697796	3 miles (4.8km)	1½ hrs	394ft (120m)
Cwmtydu	20	Cwmtydu	SN 356575	3 miles (4.8km)	1½ hrs	360ft (110m)
Devil's Bridge and the Mynach Valley	50	Devil's Bridge	SN 739769	5½ miles (8.8km)	2–3 hrs	820ft (250m)
Furnace and the Dyfi Estuary	18	Furnace	SN 684953	3 miles (4.8km)	1½ hrs	393ft (120m)
Little Quay Bay and Afon Drywi	22	Cei-bach	SN 409595	3¾ miles (5.75km)	2 hrs	426ft (130m)
Llanbadarn Fawr	29	Aberystwyth station	SN 586816	4¼ miles (6.8km)	2½ hrs	230ft (70m)
Llanerchaeron	56	Aberaeron	SN 456630	5¾ miles (9.2km)	2–2½ hrs	245ft (75m)
Llangranog and Ynys Lochtyn	26	Llangranog	SN 316538	3¾ miles (6km)	2 hrs	525ft (160m)
Llyn Brianne	74	Llyn Briane dam	SN 793485	7 miles (11.2km)	4 hrs	985ft (300m)
New Quay	83	New Quay	SN 387599	7½ miles (12km)	4 hrs	525ft (160m)
Nant-y-moch	80	Nant-y-moch Dam	SN 756862	7 miles (11.2km)	3–4 hrs	1361ft (415m)
Penbryn	47	Penbryn	SN 296522	5½ miles (8.8km)	3 hrs	508ft (155m)
Pen Dinas	12	Aberystwyth	SN 581818	3 miles (4.8km)	1½ hrs	410ft (125m)
Pen y Garn	77	The Arch	SN 766756	7 miles (11.2km)	3–4 hrs	2001ft (610m)
Plynlimon	41	Eisteddfa Gurig	SN 798841	5 miles (8km)	3 hrs	2467ft (752m)
Soar y Mynydd and the Afon Doethie	53	Soar y Mynydd	SN 784534	6 miles (9.6km)	3 hrs	1443ft (440m)
Strata Florida	44	Strata Florida	SN 746657	5 miles (8km)	2½ hrs	1115ft (340m)
Teifi Marshes and the Afon Teifi	16	Teifi Marshes Nature Reserve	SN 187450	3 miles (4.8km)	2 hrs	165ft (50m)
Teifi Pools Walk	87	Strata Florida	SN 746657	9 miles (14.5km)	4–5 hrs	1475ft (450m)
Trefechan to Morfa Bychan	62	Trefechan beach	SN 579807	6⅓ miles (10.2km)	3 hrs	443ft (135m)
Trefeurig	64	Llyn Pendam, Cwmsymlog	SN 711839	6¼ miles (10km)	3 hrs	1066ft (325m)
Tresaith and Aberporth	67	Tresaith	SN 278512	6½ miles (10.4km)	3½ hrs	410ft (125m)

Comments

Riverside walks and a lovely green lane that loops across the hillside above Aberaeron lead to the village of Aberarth before a return along the foreshore.

Coastal walking leads to a wooded ravine and the Church of St David; leafy lanes feature twice in this walk, the second ambling easily down to the banks of the Afon Aeron.

A short, sharp climb leads to a fine, airy traverse above Cardigan Bay to Clarach Bay, before a lovely cross-country return on old tracks and woodland paths.

Peaceful rurality, wandering quiet farm lanes and fields with outstanding views across the Afon Teifi to the coastline of Pembrokeshire.

A lovely switchback cliff-top walk leads south to a narrow glen. Quiet lanes and farm tracks take the walk back cross-country to Borth.

Green lanes and quiet roads lead across lush farmland to visit the abbey ruins of St Dogmaels. Peace and tranquillity are key elements in this lovely walk.

An easy circuit of the Cwm Rheidol Reservoir making use of woodland trails and path. Peace and quiet are the main reasons for this walk – that and some wonderful scenery.

Delightful quiet lanes lead to a lovely woodland path and a circuit of the cliffs to the north-east of the tiny bay of Cwmtydu.

A stiff start leads into the long and delightful valley of the Afon Mynach (The Monk's River). The going can be rugged, but the scenery never fails to excel.

A stunning promenade high above the delectable Dyfi Estuary, with a visit to an 18th-century blast furnace.

The walk starts along a coastal path above a lovely and peaceful beach then leads into a wooded valley and a quiet return along farm lanes.

A simple walk that quickly leaves Aberystwyth for the adjacent village of Llanbadarn Fawr and its lovely church, before heading back along the Rheidol and the slopes of Pen Dinas.

An easy walk along the Afon Aeron to the church of St Non and then to the National Trust's Llanerchaeron Estate.

A wooded start leads to superb coastal paths and an exploration of the promontory of Ynys Lochtyn before more sea cliffs overlooking sandy beaches lead back to Llangranog.

Walk drove roads and follow in the footsteps of an outlaw on this tour of the countryside south of Llyn Brianne.

A long and scenically spectacular clifftop walk leads into the wooded glen of Cwm Soden from where the route heads inland using field paths, roads and green lanes.

A walk with two personalities: one discovered strolling alongside the huge reservoir, and the other found on the vast, empty moorland only a short track away.

A spectacular clifftop switchback leads to the lovely village of Llangrannog and inland to the wooded Hoffnant Valley, returning along quiet lanes and woodland shade.

This walk climbs to the site of an Iron Age fort, now crowned by a monument to the Duke of Wellington.

An excellent and straightforward climb to a superb mountain viewpoint, precedes an equally agreeable descent and a visit to a 19th-century experimental farm.

A straightforward 'conquest' on the highest summit in Ceredigion, *but not for a day of poor visibility.* Tremendous views in all directions, make this walk worthwhile.

A simple but remote walk to a stunningly beautiful valley. It begins from the most remote chapel in Wales, and concludes along an old drove road.

Exploring the countryside once managed by the monks of Strata Florida, this walk samples farm fields and old green lanes before ambling back along forest trails and bridleways.

Woodland wandering alongside a sedate river provides ample opportunity for studying birdlife, but don't let birdwatching distract you from keeping an eye on the route through this tangled woodland.

A long but easy walk into the green moorland wilderness around the source of the Afon Teifi.

A lovely clifftop walk with sea breezes and birds for company, leads to quiet lanes and a gentle stroll back to Trefechan.

An undulating visit to a fascinating region where lead and silver were most productively mined; flowing green hills and vibrant valley make this a stunning walk best reserved for a clear day.

Coastal path walking links two attractive beaches and small villages before heading inland to travel green lanes and pathways.

At-a-glance...

Introduction to Ceredigion

The Devil, it is said, lives in the middle of Wales, an area that has been described as a 'Green Desert'. But to be fair, a large portion of 'mid-Wales' falls within the adjacent county of Powys, so maybe that's the bit where the Devil lives rather than here in Ceredigion.

Today, Ceredigion holds a unique position in the history and culture of Wales. It has also undergone something of an identity crisis: having been a recognised unit since the 5th century, in 1536 it transformed into Cardiganshire. Later the county became Dyfed, but between 1974 and 1996, symptomatic of the Welshness of the region, the historical name Ceredigion was revived by the district council and the name Ceredigion County Council embraced by the new unitary authority in 1996. The region of Ceredigion is named after Ceredig, the son of the 5th-century Celtic leader Cunndda, who was the leader of the northern British tribe that recaptured this area from the Irish invaders.

The present-day county stretches from Eglwys-fach in the north to Cardigan in the south, and its main towns are Aberystwyth, Aberaeron, Lampeter, Tregaron, Llandysul and Cardigan. Of the resident population of 70,000, more than half are Welsh speakers, which is not surprising because this land to the west of the Afon Teifi is a cultural core area of Wales. Here, change occurs only slowly, a characteristic of the cautiousness of the people known as 'Cardi', renowned for their grudging acceptance of change and, some would say, tight-fisted canniness.

The Norman barons, who held such influence over the growth and development of England, came to Wales in the 12th century, but their stay was brief largely due to one man, Rhys ap Gruffydd who, in 1164, won back the territory to the Royal House of Deheubarth. Of course, this is an over-

The Marina, Trefechan

simplification, but after his success Rhys settled in Aberteifi, or Cardigan, where he rebuilt the castle. Territorial battles notwithstanding, Rhys is remembered just as much for establishing the first eisteddfod, which was held in Aberteifi in 1176, and although this was not called an eisteddfod it had all the ingredients of the latter-day music and poetry festival including the Gorsedd proclamation 12 months in advance.

Ceredigion coastline near Cwm Tydu

But rather than dwell too much on the past, let's have a look at the present, at a county that has three distinct parts. First, the coastline, and a stupendous coastline it is, too. Then an amorphous inner section that is given over to sheep farming, and finally, the lumpy bit, that forms the fringe of the afforested Cambrian Mountains, rising to Pen Pumlumon Fawr, Plynlimon.

Washed by the waters of Cardigan Bay, the Ceredigion coastline stretches for 40 miles from Pembrokeshire in the south up to the Dovey Estuary. It is a coast that has everything: spectacularly rugged gorse-covered headlands jutting out into the sea, steep cliffs, small fishing villages and harbours, sandy beaches, isolated coves, and cliff-top grasslands. Just as importantly, the coast is sparsely visited, leaving visitors with the peace and quiet to explore without crowds.

Dotted along the coast are attractive coastal towns and villages, each with remarkably distinct characteristics. All provide excellent bases for exploration on foot, from the caravan and holiday home settlement of Aberporth (by no means unique in having holiday homes); the watersports paradise at diminutive Tresaith (a tiny place that many people overlook); the long, sandy beach at Penbryn backed by sand dunes and woodland trails; Llangrannog, where a spectacular walk along the cliffs leads to the National Trust promontory at Ynys Lochtyn, and the popular traditional resort at New Quay, where the most renowned Welsh poet, Dylan Thomas, moved to in 1944 to escape the London blitz. Many believe the move revitalised Thomas's poetry, and not a few of his works were influenced by the town: *Quite Early One Morning*, for example, is a recollection of an early morning stroll through New Quay, setting the foundation for *Under Milk Wood*, which is perhaps his most famous work. Centrally placed Aberystwyth is the closest you get to a traditional seaside resort with an elevated promenade and a town well-endowed with restored Edwardian and Victorian buildings, and the National Library of Wales. Surprisingly, Aberystwyth is not built on the Afon Ystwyth, but the Afon Rheidol, and so might lay reasonable claim to being called Aberrheidol, but the Ystwyth is not far away, sweeping round the great mound of Pen Dinas to flush out the harbour at Trefechan.

From here it is only a short way to Llanbadarn Fawr, now virtually a suburb of Aberystwyth, but historically and religiously of far greater significance, a fact underlined by the grandeur of the church on the site of a religious cell established by St Padarn in the 6th century.

Part of the coastline is officially designated as a Heritage Coast, which here is divided into four separate sections totalling 21 miles, including several nature reserves and marine conservation areas, a testament to the wide variety of bird and animal populations it supports. Birds to be seen include cormorant, fulmar, kittiwake, chough, raven, peregrine, and buzzard. In addition, the Cardigan Bay Special Area of Conservation itself supports a colony of more than 100 bottle-nosed dolphins. Harbour porpoises and Atlantic grey seals are frequently seen close to shore.

Inland, lie the forests of the Cambrian Mountains and the luxuriant vales of the Teifi, Rheidol, Aeron and Ystwyth rivers which feature some truly memorable landscapes. The Afon Tiefi, which runs through three counties – Pembrokeshire, Ceredigion and Carmarthenshire – is one of only two rivers in Wales where the coracle – a small boat made from animal hide,

St David's Church, Aberarth

wrapped round a wicker structure – is still used for fishing. The Rheidol has been harnessed to provide hydroelectric power for Aberystwyth, and, with the possible exception of the huge dam at Nant-y-moch Reservoir, tastefully and sensitively so. Elsewhere, the landscape is one of green valleys, pastures edged by mature hedgerows dotted with wild flowers, and the dark intrusions of conifer plantations. Even so, this is delightful countryside to walk: red kite country, a place of hidden cwms, streams and waterfalls, ruined cottages and farms.

Along the boundary of Ceredigion with Powys rise the uplands of Plynlimon, or Pumlumon, across which strode George Borrow in his marathon journey through *Wild Wales*. Unlike Borrow, many early visitors to the area around Plynlimon displayed great anxiety and a reluctance to venture too far from the safety of the roads and settlements. Maybe this was to do with the fact the Plynlimon holds a significant place in Welsh history, as a scene of turmoil. Its grey-green bogs and shambolic terrain have witnessed many a struggle. An exterminating warfare was carried on here between Owain Cyfeilog, Prince of Powys, and Hywel ap Cadogan. Here it was, too, that Owain Glyndwr unfurled the banner of Welsh independence, and hence in the summer of 1401 harassed the adjacent countryside, sacked Montgomery, burned Welshpool and destroyed the abbey at Cwmhir.

But the greatest feature of Plymlinon must surely be its role as the mother of rivers, for it provides the wherewithal for five rivers, including the Severn, the Wye and the Rheidol, all flowing great distances to the sea and providing along the way some of the most fertile and beautiful countryside in the whole of Wales, much of which is explored in this book.
• *Glossary of Welsh Words – page 92.*

With the introduction of **'gps enabled' walks,** you will see that this book now includes a list of waypoints alongside the description of the walk. We have included these so that you can enjoy the full benefits of gps should you wish to. Gps is an amazingly useful and entertaining navigational aid, and you do not need to be computer literate to enjoy it.

GPS waypoint co-ordinates add value to your walk. You will now have the extra advantage of introducing 'direction' into your walking which will enhance your leisure walking and make it safer. Use of a gps brings greater confidence and security and you will find you cover ground a lot faster should you need to.

For essential information on map reading and basic navigation, read the *Pathfinder Guide Map Reading Skills* by outdoor writer, Terry Marsh (ISBN 978-0-7117-4978-8). For more information on using your gps, read the *Pathfinder Guide GPS for Walkers*, by gps teacher and navigation trainer, Clive Thomas (ISBN 978-0-7117-4445-5). Both titles are available in bookshops or can be ordered online at www.totalwalking.co.uk

Pen Dinas

		GPS waypoints
Start	Aberystwyth	🥾 SN 581 818
Distance	3 miles (4.8km)	**A** SN 585 810
Approximate time	1½ hours	**B** SN 588 799
Parking	Aberystwyth	**C** SN 581 806
Refreshments	Cafés, pubs and restaurants in Aberystwyth	
Ordnance Survey maps	Landranger 135 (Aberystwyth & Machynlleth), Explorer 213 (Aberystwyth & Cwm Rheidol)	

The modest summit of Pen Dinas, sandwiched between the Afon Ystwyth, on which the town of Aberystwyth is not built, and the Afon Rheidol, on which it is, provides a splendid viewpoint both over the town and inland to the hills and mountains of central Wales. This walk climbs to the site of an Iron Age fort, now crowned by a monument to the Duke of Wellington.

Aberystwyth has long been the undisputed capital of central Wales. What it loses in size, compared with Cardiff, it certainly makes up for in the culture and traditions of Wales. Students and holidaymakers maintain a constant buzz in the town, whatever the time of year.

🥾 From the promenade turn into the town and leave along the A487, signposted for Cardigan. The road soon crosses the Rheidol on a bridge where in

Allt Wen and Cardigan Bay from Pen Dinas

1963, Cymdeithas yr Iaith Gymraeg (the Welsh Language Society) held its first non-violent protest for equality for the Welsh language.

The road continues through the suburb of Trefechan and soon passes the fire station. Stay along the main road as far as a signposted footpath on the right (just where the road speed limit increases to 40mph) **A**. Keep to the right of a metal gate onto a path gently rising to a wooden kissing-gate beyond which it continues into light woodland cover.

At a second kissing-gate, turn right alongside a hedgerow, parallel with a rough stony track. The path climbs to a third, much larger, kissing-gate, and then curves round passing through the hill-fort defences and onto the summit of Pen Dinas and its towering monument. Raised by public subscription, this was built around 1852 in memory of the Duke of Wellington, victor at Waterloo.

Go past the monument, following a grassy path which soon starts to descend quite steeply. Keep following the descending path through a spread of bell heather and sheep's-bit scabious, but when this bears sharply right and continues steeply downwards, leave it by going forward at a more gentle gradient to reach a fence corner. Here, the path bends right and left heading towards modern housing.

Just before a wooden kissing-gate **B**, turn abruptly right, descending beside a fence and an old wall overgrown with blackthorn and bramble. The path descends through an area of disused working, waymarked by poles and seasonally overgrown, and soon joins a broad track. Common mallow, montbretia, buddleia, hawkweed, ragwort and willowherb grow in profusion here. In medieval times, when there was widespread faith in the efficacy of love potions, mallow was sometimes a saving grace as it had a reputation as an anti-aphrodisiac.

The ongoing track finally becomes a surfaced lane and is followed until it reaches more housing **C**. Here, turn left onto a signposted path that leads around the end of houses and along a path enclosed by high privet hedgerows.

Finally, the path emerges at a road beside the harbour. Follow the road for a short distance and then branch left

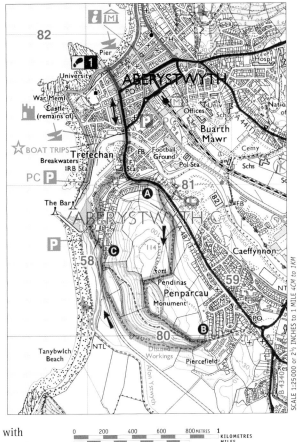

along a wide, dirt track at the harbour edge. Follow the water's edge and soon enter the marina area alongside harbour-front properties to emerge at the back of the fire station. Nearby stands one of only two remaining lime kilns that were built along the coast around Aberystwyth. The kilns were placed close to the harbour because limestone and coal had to be imported from South Wales. The heat given off from the kilns made them a place of popular resort and they became public meeting places where children gathered to roast potatoes and listen to the tales spun by the lime burners.

At the nearby road junction, turn left to recross the Rheidol bridge and return to Aberystwyth. ●

Cwm Rheidol

Start	Cwm Rheidol Reservoir Visitor Centre	**GPS waypoints**	
Distance	3 miles (4.8km)	SN 697 796	
Approximate time	1½ hours	Ⓐ SN 711 785	
Parking	Adjacent Visitor Centre	Ⓑ SN 709 780	
Refreshments	Visitor Centre (light refreshments only)	Ⓒ SN 709 784	
Ordnance Survey maps	Landranger 135 (Aberystwyth & Machynlleth), Explorer 213 (Aberystwyth & Cwm Rheidol)		

It is always heartening to find man-made intrusions into a natural environment that do not look man-made. This is very much the case with the Cwm Rheidol Reservoir, the lowest of three reservoirs that form the Rheidol Scheme, harnessing the power of the Afon Rheidol. This is all the more important because the Rheidol is a breeding area for salmon and trout. The valley is also a place favoured by red kite that can often be seen circling overhead, although the sound of the Vale of Rheidol Railway, a delightful excursion from Aberystwyth, can rather take you by surprise. But its passing by is only a moment in an otherwise peaceful and serene setting. It is these qualities of peacefulness and serenity that are the hallmark of this walk, which, in essence, circles the reservoir.

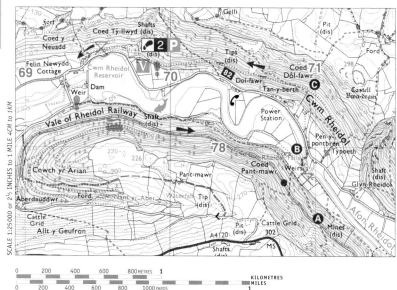

SCALE 1:25 000 or 2½ INCHES to 1 MILE 4CM to 1KM

| 0 | 200 | 400 | 600 | 800 METRES | 1 |
| 0 | 200 | 400 | 600 | 800 | 1000 YARDS |

KILOMETRES
MILES
1

Cwm Rheidol landscape

🖉 From the visitor centre car park walk back along the road and take the turning on the left (signposted to Aberffrwd). When the road bends right, leave it by branching left through a gate onto a broad forest trail.

Keep following the forest trail which climbs steadily above the Afon Rheidol and, at the bottom edge of Coed Pant-mawr, continue, with improving views up the valley, as far as an obvious ravine with a waterfall on the opposite side of the valley. Roughly opposite this, look for a green path **Ⓐ** slanting backwards from (and above) the forest trail, and turn sharply left, going down to a step-stile across a fence.

Over the stile, bear left alongside the fence, but only as far as another stile, and here head down-field to a stile at a fence corner. Over this follow an enclosed path to a footbridge spanning the river, and, on the other side, walk up to meet a lane **Ⓑ**.

Turn right as far as the turning to Ty Poeth, and here go left onto a signposted access track leading to a cottage. At the cottage, go forward through a gate and onto a steep path rising into woodland, where the on-going path immediately forks. Branch left (waymark) and climb steadily into the woodland. The path swings right at another waymark, and a short way above this, leave the main path by crossing a fence stile on the left to gain a brief path that leads up to a broad forest trail **Ⓒ**.

Turn left onto the trail and, with occasional views across the valley to the railway and up-river, follow it back to the visitor centre. ●

Teifi Marshes and the Afon Teifi

Start	Teifi Marsh	**GPS waypoints**	
Distance	3 miles (4.8km)	🥾 SN 187 450	
Approximate time	2 hours	Ⓐ SN 194 445	
		Ⓑ SN 189 440	
Parking	Teifi Marsh Nature Reserve	Ⓒ SN 191 432	
Refreshments	Visitor Centre café	Ⓓ SN 188 437	
Ordnance Survey maps	Landranger 145 (Cardigan & Mynydd Preseli), Explorer 198 (Cardigan & New Quay)		

Clinging to the Afon Teifi, which here is the border between Ceredigion and Pembrokeshire, this walk explores the lush woodland that flanks the river before returning from a point just north of Cilgerran. The way is clear throughout, but in the tangled woodland there is plenty of opportunity for going astray before Cilgerran is reached. At the start, the Teifi Marshes offer a series of trails that take in the wide diversity of this splendid habitat which is especially rich in birdlife at all times of the year.

🥾 From the car park walk to the visitor centre and then turn onto the Otter Trail, a surfaced path. Shortly, turn right for the 'Viewpoint'. Just before the viewpoint, turn right once again onto the Gorge Trail, which then sets off up this splendid river valley.

The steep-sided gorge carrying the River Teifi was cut through the hillside here at the end of the last Ice Age, about 10,000 years ago. The woodland on the far bank is one of the largest remaining areas of the ancient forest that once covered much of Wales.

The Gorge Trail reaches another small viewing platform where the surfacing ends Ⓐ, after which it presses on as a narrow woodland footpath, occasionally overgrown, until it finally stops at the foot of steps. Between these two points the path forks: take the right branch, climbing away from the river to reach the steps.

The ongoing route

Canoeing on the Afon Teifi

now negotiates a series of steps, some up, some down, that take the path up to the top edge of the woodland where the path eventually leads to a stile giving onto a broad, shaded track above the gorge.

The track emerges eventually near a couple of metal gates not far from the deserted farm at Forest **B**. Here, go left over a stile descending back into woodland, although the path generally keeps to the higher ground. Hitherto, the woodland has been mainly broad-leaved, but for a while the narrow, twisting, overgrown path gives way to a broad track on pine needles as the route passes through a larch plantation. The route is now waymarked. Keep an eye open for a waymark sending the path to the right, just after the second footbridge.

The larch plantation is relatively short and gives into more scrubby woodland before popping out at a stile near a large field. Turn into the field and go forward along the left-hand edge to locate a stile in the far corner. Over this, turn right onto a surfaced lane, but follow it only as far as the next footpath signpost on the right. Here **C**, turn onto a gated vehicle track between houses.

Progress now significantly improves, but before reaching Forest Farm, keep a lookout for a signposted path on the left (the signpost is on the right), which dives back into woodland **D**. The path descends steadily and passes a derelict building,

shortly after which it meets a gate. Just before the gate turn up to the right to find the continuing path, which now runs along the bottom edge of woodland, with rough pasture on the left.

The woodland path is easier to follow than its counterpart above the Afon Teifi. At a stile it re-enters the Teifi Marshes Nature Reserve. When the on-going path meets the Squirrel Trail, where the track forks, branch left, passing a cottage to reach the Otter Trail which leads down to a road. Turn right to return to the car park. ●

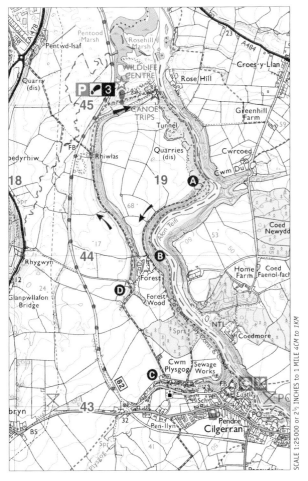

Furnace and the Dyfi Estuary

		GPS waypoints
Start	Furnace	
Distance	3 miles (4.8km)	SN 684 953
Approximate time	1½ hours	**A** SN 684 948
Parking	Furnace (free)	**B** SN 691 947
Refreshments	Machynlleth	**C** SN 693 961
Ordnance Survey maps	Landranger 135 (Aberystwyth & Machynlleth), Explorer OL23 (Cadair Idris & Llyn Tegid)	

The abundance of forest woodland and a fast-flowing river were the essential ingredients sought by any 18th-century iron-making company, and it was this that brought Vernon, Kendall and Company to this northern edge of Ceredigion. This walk begins with a visit to the blast furnace, before making a splendid traverse of the craggy slopes of Foel Fawr. You can extend the walk by a visit to the Ynys-hir RSPB Nature Reserve, which contains one of the most important heronries in Wales.

Dyfi Furnace, which gave the tiny village its name, was an iron-producing blast furnace built in about 1755, but it was only in production for 50 years, and had been abandoned by 1810. It was later converted into a sawmill, and the present waterwheel, although restored, belongs to this time. The furnace at Dyfi was fired by charcoal from the surrounding woodlands, and the blast was powered by water diverted from the river. Most of the iron it produced went to forges in the Midlands.

Walk out from the CADW car park to the main road. The renowned furnace stands opposite and is well worth a visit.

Turn right and then immediately left onto a narrow lane signposted to Cwm Einion and the Artists' Valley. Climb the lane, but as it bends sharply to the left **A**, leave it by going forward on a signposted footpath, a stony track rising into woodland.

The heather and crags of Foel Fawr

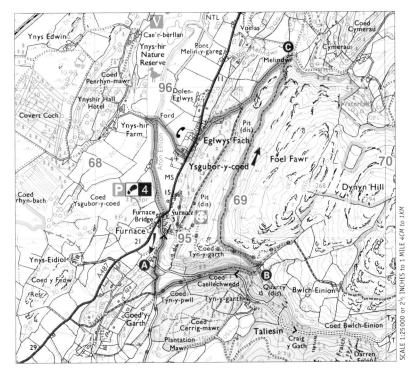

The woodland path climbs to meet a farm track. Turn left along this, from which there is a lovely view over the Dyfi Valley. The track gently descends to meet a surfaced lane. Go forward along the lane, as far as a signposted path descending left as a broad track into woodland. This is a delightful path that descends to cross the Afon Einion by a footbridge **B**.

On the other side climb to, but do not cross, a nearby stile. Instead, bear left onto a rising path that leads to a gate giving onto an access track near a cottage. Turn left and walk up to meet a surfaced lane at a footpath signpost.

Bear left but only for a short distance, leaving the track by turning right at a sign onto a grassy path ascending through bracken across the crag and heather slopes of Foel Fawr with an ever-improving view over the wide expanse of the Dyfi Estuary. At the high point of the walk, the path passes a small rocky outcrop on which there is a small view indicator overlooking the Ynys-Hir Estate. The path is a delightful promenade with impressive views both of the estuary and the Tarren Hills beyond Machynlleth.

When the path divides, keep forward, taking the higher branch. Eventually, it descends quite steeply to meet a lane **C** near Melindwr Farm. Here turn left. At a cattle-grid, the lane enters light woodland of birch and oak, and continues down to meet the main road. Turn left and, *taking care against approaching traffic*, walk as far as the side road leading to the Ynys-hir Hall Hotel and RSPB reserve. Here, leave the main road and walk down to cross the Afon Einion, and a short way farther on, opposite the entrance to the hotel grounds, turn sharply left at a cottage, and follow a riverside track back to the CADW car park at Furnace. ●

Cwmtydu

		GPS waypoints
Start	Cwmtydu Bay	 SN 356 575
Distance	3 miles (4.8km)	**A** SN 365 568
Approximate time	1½ hours	**B** SN 372 569
Parking	Cwmtydu Bay	**C** SN 367 577
Refreshments	Café at Cwmtydu	**D** SN 364 580
Ordnance Survey maps	Landranger 145 (Cardigan & Mynydd Preseli), Explorer 198 (Cardigan & New Quay)	

Tucked away down narrow lanes, the coastal hamlet of Cwmtydu is charming and carries no trace of the business of smuggling that once went on here and in adjacent sea caves. In fact, this was quite a hive of industry, apart from smuggling. Legitimate cargoes of limestone would arrive from south Wales for burning in the kiln still standing near the water's edge, and farmers would travel down the valley to collect burned lime to spread on their fields as fertiliser.

Leave Cwmtydu by walking up the road for about 660 yds (600m). Although the road is used by cars going down to the beach, the traffic is light and the road is flanked by broad-leaved trees and every step of the way accompanied by the sound of running water. Take the first turning, a minor road, on the left. Follow this to a junction and bear right, continuing to another junction where the road bends

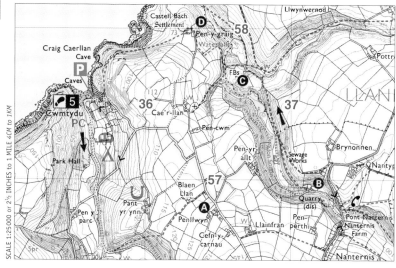

SCALE 1:25 000 or 2½ INCHES to 1 MILE 4CM to 1KM

Heading into Cwm Soden

right (signposted for Caerwedros). Continue to a turning just before a small postbox **A**. Turn left here and keep following the road past Pen-yr-allt, after which the road narrows and descends into woodland.

Head down to a bridge spanning the Afon Soden **B**. Over the bridge, turn left to a metal gate, and shortly branch right to a stile giving onto a rising path. This turns out to be a lovely path shrouded by trees, but eventually comes down to a wooden kissing-gate at the entrance to the National Trust's Cwm Soden estate. Beyond the gate the path crosses a small clearing before descending into woodland once more.

Shortly after entering the woodland, the path descends to a footbridge **C**. Ignore this and branch left on a stony path signposted to 'Cwmtudu'. The path shortly reaches another footbridge. [*A flight of steps to the left of the bridge leads up to a path that runs out to the 13th-century church of St Tysilio.*] Over the bridge, turn right, following the path as it climbs to a gate. Just after the gate, bear left into a sloping pasture and walk to its top right-hand corner. Turn through a gate to a track junction and

there turn right to reach Pen-y-graig Farm **D**. Keep to the right of the farm, passing through a gate and walking away on a broad track that soon swings left and passes above the Iron Age site at Castell Bach.

Pass above a small bay, and from a kissing-gate climb onto the headland from where the path runs round to reach Cwmtydu. When it forks, branch right, following a steeply descending path to meet a road near the tiny beach. ●

The beautiful Ceredigion coastline from the Coastal Path near Cwmtydu

Little Quay Bay and Afon Drywi

Start	Cei-bach
Distance	3¾ miles (5.75km)
Approximate time	2 hours
Parking	Cei-bach Beach
Refreshments	New Quay
Ordnance Survey maps	Landranger 146 (Lampeter & Llandovery), Explorer 198 (Cardigan & New Quay)

GPS waypoints

- 🖊 SN 409 595
- Ⓐ SN 415 598
- Ⓑ SN 426 607
- Ⓒ SN 428 605
- Ⓓ SN 428 600
- Ⓔ SN 417 594

While New Quay bustles with its teeming visitors, its near neighbour, Cei-bach, or Little Quay Bay, has long, sandy beaches that are virtually empty. This short walk skips along above the beach and then turns inland along the course of Afon Drywi before climbing out for the return along farm lanes and tracks.

🖊 From the car park, cross the road and walk forward to a white house. There, turn left through a kissing-gate onto a hedgerowed path that leads to a stile giving into a steeply sloping pasture. Keep forward along the bottom of the slope and go past a hedge gap and continue to a field corner stile. Beyond, maintain the same direction, giving onto a woodland path that runs on

Sunset at Little Quay Bay

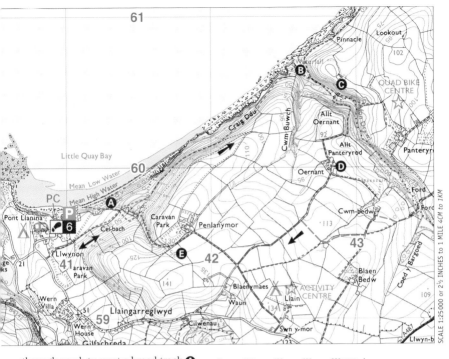

SCALE 1:25 000 or 2½ INCHES to 1 MILE 4CM to 1KM

through scrub to meet a broad track **A**. Go left and almost immediately right, continuing on a signposted grassy path that climbs steadily above Little Quay Bay and Craig Ddu.

At a wooden gate, the path continues across a wooded slope and then assumes a delightful and gently rising traverse of sea slopes. Gradually, the path starts to descend as it approaches Cwm Drywi. Cross a stile and go down to cross the Afon Drywi **B**. On the other side walk up to a signpost and there turn right onto a track heading up the valley.

Continue as far as a waymark pole on the right **C**, just before the valley track swings left. Here, go down to a shallow ford and continue up a stony track on the other side, climbing through woodland. When the track forks, take the higher option, climbing to the top edge of woodland. There, cross a stile and go forward along an overgrown sunken track that leads to a stile near a gate.

Walk up a green lane leading up to a

farm **D**. Keep to the right of the farm buildings to a step-stile giving onto a surfaced access lane. Follow the lane as far as the turning to Penlanymor Caravan Park. Turn right here, and just before the entrance to the caravan park, bear left along a stony track.

Just past the far end of the caravan site, pass through a gate across the track, then immediately right through a second gate **E** onto a descending track, then half-right to another gate lower down. Cross a stream bed and climb up to a track coming out of the caravan site, and turn left following the descending track through peaceful woodland.

Keep descending until the track meets the pathway used earlier in the walk, at a signpost **A**. Here, turn left and retrace the outward route to the white house, turning right there to return to the car park.

Cardigan and St Dogmaels Abbey

		GPS waypoints
Start	Cardigan	📝 SN 156 460
Distance	4 miles (6.4km)	**Ⓐ** SN 175 456
Approximate time	2 hours	**Ⓑ** SN 161 448
Parking	Cardigan (Quay Street)	**Ⓒ** SN 161 452
Refreshments	Cardigan	
Ordnance Survey maps	Landranger 145 (Cardigan & Mynydd Preseli), Explorer 198 (Cardigan & New Quay)	

Most of the land south of the Afon Teifi, at least near its estuary, lies outside Ceredigion. Near St Dogmaels, however, Ceredigion seems to have filched a wedge of Pembrokeshire. Mostly it is farmland, which this walk wanders quietly through before stepping over into the neighbouring county to visit the abbey ruins at St Dogmaels.

Since the Teifi Valley is very much the standard-bearer of the Welsh woollen industry, it is only a short step to assume that the bustling town of Cardigan owes its name to that woollen garment of the same name. In fact, the originator was the 7th Earl of Cardigan, renowned for his gallantry in leading the attack on Balaclava during the Crimean War.

📝 There is a sizeable car park at the end of Quay Street (near the supermarket), and from it walk up to the main road and turn right, going down towards the river, crossing it by a foot-bridge along-side the town's ancient arched bridge. A short way on, turn right onto the B4546 for St Dogmaels. Shortly take the signposted bridleway on the left which rises gently as a vehicle track serving the cottage at Parc-y-pys **Ⓐ**. Here, keep forward into scrub, and then along a tree-shaded pathway beside a stream.

Continue up to Parc-yr-eithin Farm,

there crossing a track at gates and going forward to a stile beside a metal gate. Beyond, keep on along a broad field track, rising gently around the edge of a pasture.

The track comes out to meet a road. Turn right and continue as far as a signposted bridleway opposite Plas Newydd, a house on the right. Leave the road here and head along a surfaced lane to pass cottages and then continue to Cefn Uchaf, where the road surfacing ends. From there continue along a hedgerowed green lane flanked by luxuriant growths of hart's tongue fern and lady-fern, as well as ivy-strangled hawthorns and hazel.

The track emerges at Blaenwaun Baptist Chapel **Ⓑ**, an austere building at the top end of a large graveyard. Go past the chapel to meet a lane at a bend, and there keep forward, shortly bearing right around the graveyard boundary wall. At the lower entrance to the graveyard, a slate warns visitors to the church about disfiguring monuments, taking flowers 'or other unseemly acts'.

The road comes down to a T-junction. Turn left but very soon leave the road by turning right onto a signposted path **C** which takes the route briefly into Pembrokeshire as it first climbs and then contours above Cwm Degwel. The path is a delightful, shaded green lane that leads unerringly to St Dogmaels, allowing a couple of elevated views of the abbey ruins.

Looking down on the ruins of St Dogmaels Abbey

At a lane, turn right and follow the lane down to a T-junction. Turn right again, and at Church Street, divert to pay a visit to the impressive ruins of the abbey. The abbey was a daughter house of the French Abbey of Tiron and was founded in the 12th century.

Leave the abbey and go back to the main road, following this down to pass the White Hart Inn, and then keep on along the B-road back to the old bridge to conclude the walk. ●

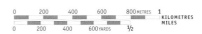

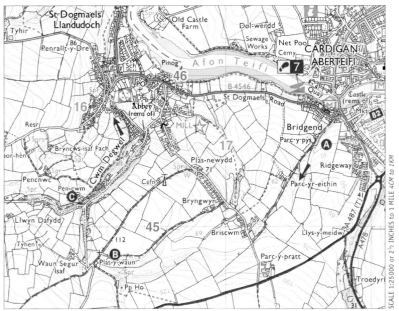

Llangranog and Ynys Lochtyn

		GPS waypoints	
Start	Llangranog	🖉	SN 316 538
Distance	3¾ miles (6km)	Ⓐ	SN 327 541
Approximate time	2 hours	Ⓑ	SN 324 549
Parking	Llangranog (free)	Ⓒ	SN 316 548
Refreshments	Pubs and cafés in Llangranog	Ⓓ	SN 314 549
Ordnance Survey maps	Landranger 145 (Cardigan & Mynydd Preseli), Explorer 198 (Cardigan & New Quay)	Ⓔ	SN 316 540

The allure of Ynys Lochtyn should not be underestimated. The walk, which begins along a shady woodland passage, swings round to confront the hill fort of Pen y Badell and the promontory of Ynys Lochtyn, the final bit of which is a tidal island – attainable, with care and an eye on the tide. Harbour porpoise and bottle-nosed dolphins frequent the waters here, along with Atlantic grey seals, and Ynys Lochtyn proves to be a good vantage point to look for them. But sea watching is a time-consuming pastime, and no allowance has been given for this. Today, Llangranog is a popular beach resort, but scratch its surface and a much shadier past is revealed.

🖉 The parking down near the beach in Llangranog is limited, so this walk starts from a signposted car park along a narrow lane above the post office. *Bus services do run down to the beach and anyone arriving by this means should begin there and walk up the road to the car park.*

From the car park turn right and head up the road, turning with it as it bends left and then, just before it swings very sharply right, leaving the road for a footpath descending along the base of a wooded slope. When the path is crossed by another, keep forward taking the lower option and eventually emerge at Pigeonsford Farm. Walk out along the access to a road and there turn left Ⓐ.

Follow the road past the walled garden at Pigeonsford, climbing steadily to a road junction. Cross into the road opposite (signposted for the ski slope). As the road bends left leave it by crossing a step-stile on the right beside a double metal gate, and turn onto a path parallel with the road, which it soon rejoins at the entrance to the Urdd Centre. The centre was opened by the Welsh League of Youth in 1932, and caters for thousands of visitors annually. It provides courses and activity holidays for Welsh-speaking children and learners with the aim of promoting the Welsh language and culture. The Urdd is a dynamic youth movement with a membership of more than 45,000, which

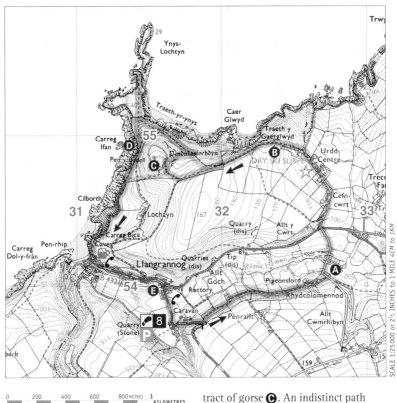

SCALE 1:25 000 or 2½ INCHES to 1 MILE 4CM to 1KM

```
0        200      400      600      800 METRES   1
                                        KILOMETRES
                                        MILES
0        200      400      600 YARDS       ½
```

organises its own annual eisteddfod, the largest youth festival in Europe.

Keep forward towards the ski slope, and near its entrance branch right down a fenced track which soon ends at a stile giving onto the coastal path. Turn onto this, climbing above sea cliffs. After a short rise, which brings Ynys Lochtyn into view, the path descends briefly to a stile from which a clear path runs along the seaward side of a fence and earthbank. From the high ground **B** there is a fine view northwards along the coast to the Lleyn Peninsula more then 40 miles (65km) away, Bardsey Island and the summits of Snowdonia among which Cadair Idris is prominent.

The coastal path descends to a gate. Here, bear right onto a track rising onto Pen y Badell, a shapely hill decked in gorse and heather. Soon leave the track, by bearing right down the edge of a tract of gorse **C**. An indistinct path goes down to meet a clearer path below, which in turn swings around Pen y Badell, now heading for Ynys Lochtyn. When the path forks, branch right, taking the lower path and descending to a point giving access to the promontory. Turn down onto it and explore at leisure. The main, non-island, part of the promontory has some lovely inlets and sea arches, and most visitors should be content with exploring this. The English composer, Edward Elgar took a holiday near here in 1902 and enjoyed wandering the sea cliffs. It was while doing so on one occasion that he overheard people singing on the beach near Ynys Lochtyn, and this inspired one of his most popular and moving compositions, the *Introduction and Allegro* for strings.

A clear, broad green path runs up the middle of the promontory, and this should be used to continue the walk, ascending to meet a horizontal path contouring across the seaward slope of Pen y Badell. Leave the path at a gate on the right **ⓓ** giving onto a narrow path descending through bracken and then skimming along above sea cliffs before finally going down to the sheltered cove at Llangranog. Here turn left up the main road, passing the Ship Inn, with its lovely mural of a pirate ship, a link with a dubious past, although there was a good trade, too, in building large wooden sailing ships.

Continue up the road, climbing all the time to reach a turning, near St Carnog's Church **ⓔ** for Brynhoffnant. Turn right and walk past the post office, continuing up to return to the car park and the end of the walk. ●

The beach near Ynys Lochtyn

Llanbadarn Fawr

Start	Aberystwyth station	**GPS waypoints**	
Distance	4¼ miles (6.8km)	SN 586 816	
Approximate time	2½ hours	**A** SN 594 809	
		B SN 602 804	
Parking	Aberystwyth	**C** SN 592 801	
Refreshments	Aberystwyth, Llanbadarn Fawr	**D** SN 581 805	
Ordnance Survey maps	Landranger 135 (Aberystwyth & Machynlleth), Explorer 213 (Aberystwyth & Cwm Rheidol)		

This short walk from Aberystwyth visits the adjacent village, now almost a suburb, of Llanbadarn Fawr, which boasts a splendid church. A brief encounter with the Afon Rheidol leads to a final climb across the slopes of Pen Dinas and an easy stroll back from Trefechan marina into Aberystwyth.

From the railway station in Aberystwyth, turn right and shortly go right through metal gates onto a lovely boulevard, Plas Crug, that leads past the clutter of domestic Aberystwyth to a school. Turn right at the school and walk up to, but not across, the railway. At the railway crossing, bear left on a path flanked by butterfly-favoured shrubbery, and walk past two rugby fields to reach a wooden kissing-gate **A**.

From the gate, cross the edge of a playing field to a gate giving onto the back of a modern building, and walk out along a surfaced lane to meet the A44. Turn right, and, at the turning to Llanbadarn Fawr village, branch left to visit the lovely church with its stout tower and unusual pyramid on top.

The church was founded by St Padarn, a contemporary of St David, and it quickly grew to

become a prominent centre of early monasticism, retaining an abbot for many years. The present building, which largely replaces one destroyed by the Vikings, dates mainly from the 12th century, and is one of the largest churches in Wales.

Go past the church to a road junction, and turn right, crossing the A44, and walking down the road signposted to Cardigan (Aberteifi). Cross the main line

The Cwm Rheidol Railway at Llanbadarn Fawr

railway and that of the Cwm Rheidol narrow-gauge railway beyond. Immediately after the narrow gauge railway, turn left to a metal kissing-gate, and go forward along a broad stony track that leads to a bridge spanning the Afon Rheidol **B**. At the bridge turn right on a surfaced pathway that accompanies the river, and finally reaches the A4120. Climb up steps to the right of a bridge to reach the road.

Turn left, and cross the road with care. Walk uphill towards a roundabout at the junction with the A487. Just before the roundabout, bear right along the edge of a playing area, finally emerging onto the A487 near a pedestrian crossing **C**.

Cross into the road opposite (footpath signpost), and opposite a pub, turn right onto a rising lane leading to Parc Dinas. At a mini-roundabout, turn right into Parc Dinas, climbing past houses as far as a footpath signpost on the right for a Local Nature Reserve. Turn right here and soon cross a stile, walking up a path to meet a higher track. Cross to a kissing-gate, and then take the rising path ahead, which climbs onto Pen Dinas.

When the path forks, keep to the lower path, which soon levels and contours across the slopes of Pen Dinas,

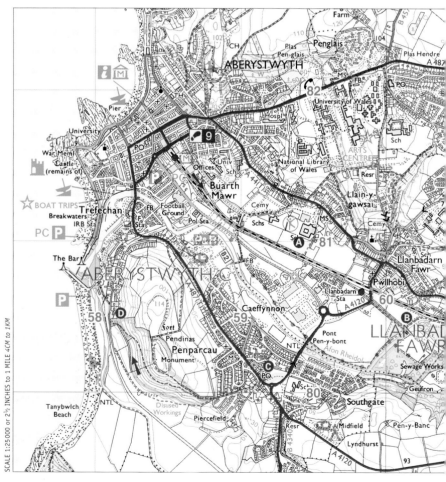

SCALE 1:25 000 or 2½ INCHES to 1 MILE 4CM to 1KM

with outstanding views southwards of the coastal hills and the lush farmlands behind them.

From another kissing-gate the path gradually descends, later going down a section where it is closely flanked by hedgerows, before emerging onto a rough lane, at the edge of modern housing Ⓓ. Here, turn right, and soon go left onto a signposted path that leads around the end of houses and along a path enclosed by high privet hedgerows.

Finally, the path emerges at a road beside the harbour. Follow the road for a short distance and then branch left along a wide, dirt track at the harbour edge. Follow the water's edge and soon enter the marina area alongside harbour-front properties to emerge at the back of the fire station. At the nearby road junction, turn left to recross the Rheidol bridge and then turn right into Mill Street to return to Aberystwyth. ●

The Afon Rheidol

Aber Teifi

		GPS waypoints
Start	Cardigan	🖉 SN 156 460
Distance	4¼ miles (6.8km)	Ⓐ SN 174 468
Approximate time	2 hours	Ⓑ SN 169 482
Parking	Cardigan (Quay Street)	Ⓒ SN 177 475
Refreshments	Cardigan	
Ordnance Survey maps	Landranger 145 (Cardigan & Mynydd Preseli), Explorer 198 (Cardigan & New Quay)	

This uncomplicated walk has more to do with the views of the Teifi at its estuary than the town, hence 'Aber Teifi' rather than 'Aberteifi', which is the proper name for the town. There are a couple of long road-walking sections: one is peaceful and quiet, being no more than farm lanes, the other is not, since it is the main road to a caravan site overlooking Poppit Sands. Elsewhere, the scene is pure rurality where even the cows are too relaxed to bother moving as you pass by. The views across the Teifi to the coastline of Pembrokeshire are outstanding, but the variety of birdlife and the number of butterflies among the hedgerows are also good reasons for taking on this unassuming little walk.

Cardigan is a bright and bustling place, but never quite succeeds in shrugging off the impression that it is rather withdrawn from the world – nor need it do so. It is a peaceful place with a remarkable bridge, and until it came under the scrutiny of Edward I, was successful in retaining a strong sense of

The Afon Teifi at Cardigan

SCALE 1:25000 or 2½ INCHES to 1 MILE 4CM to 1KM

Welshness. There was a time when Cardigan commanded a considerable amount of trade across the Irish Sea, but today it remains a solid base for everything that is intrinsically Welsh.

Cross the Quay Street car park to the far side and enter a riverside lawned area, before branching up and right onto a surfaced pathway. Follow the path round an octagonal shelter still following the surfaced path to meet a lane. Turn left. At the end of the road branch left on an enclosed path alongside a Water Treatment Plant.

From a wooden kissing-gate the path continues below an arable field and above a steep slope to the river. At a stile, cross into an adjacent field and go forward along its left-hand edge to reach Old Castle Farm. Here, turn right onto a lane (Old Castle Road). Follow the lane to a T-junction, and there turn left.

When the road next bends left at signpost 13 **A** near a bench, turn left, sheltered by high hedgerows that harbour honeysuckle, red campion, herb robert and willowherb. As the road next bends left, leave it by going forward on

ABER TEIFI ● 33

a dirt track to a metal gate beside which a wooden gate gives onto a delightful path passing along the bottom edge of a field, with improving views ahead of the Teifi Estuary and Poppit Sands.

A corner gate gives into an arable field. Maintain the same direction to another gate and then across a small pasture to a corner gate. From here follow the ongoing path until it encounters a step-stile on the left. Cross this for a brief skirmish with scrubby woodland, at the end of which the path emerges back into the field just left.

Follow the fence boundary and walk out to meet a road at a double gate **B**. Turn right and follow the roadside footpath. When this ends, *take care against approaching traffic*, and walk along the road, leaving it just after another road joins from the left **C**.

Turn right onto a signposted footpath that goes up a surfaced lane. As the road bends to the right, near a new house, leave it on the bend by going forward through a narrow wooden gate and along the gable of the house to a stile.

Keep on in the same direction in the ensuing field to reach a stile and gate giving access to a broad track that leads into a large field. Maintain the same direction and finally emerge to rejoin the lane used in the early part of the walk at signpost 13 **A**.

Keep forward and go past the turning to Old Castle Farm, following the lane as it descends into Cardigan. Turn sharply right around the edge of a car park near the Indoor Market. Take the first turning on the right, which will lead back to the Quay Street car park. ●

Poppit Sands, Aber Teifi

Aberaeron to Aberarth

		GPS waypoints
Start	Aberaeron	📷 SN 456 630
Distance	4¼ miles (6.8km)	**A** SN 464 625
Approximate time	2 hours	**B** SN 476 633
Parking	Aberaeron	**C** SN 479 637
Refreshments	Cafés, pubs and restaurants in Aberaeron	**D** SN 476 638
Ordnance Survey maps	Landranger 146 (Lampeter & Llandovery), Explorer 198 (Cardigan & New Quay)	

It seems a shame to leave the lovely harbour town of Aberaeron, with its colourful houses and bright bustling atmosphere, but this walk takes time to make the acquaintance of the town's river, the Afon Aeron, and to dawdle along lovely old lanes high on the hillside above the town. The turning point is the small village of Aberarth, one of the earliest settlements along Cardigan Bay, from which the return is along the foreshore. Before setting off, you need to check tide tables by asking at the tourist information office, otherwise you risk lengthy detours along a busy road. *But most of the time, this is not a problem, and time can be spent keeping an eye open for the bird and marine life that populates the coastline.*

In the early 19th century, the Reverend Alban Thomas Jones Gwynne, the principal landowner hereabouts, was given permission to build two piers at the mouth of the Afon Aeron. The effect was to transform what was an attractive fishing village into a thriving ship-building economy and herring fishing port. With such prosperity, the village saw a rapid growth of new residential and commercial properties built in the Regency and Georgian styles, producing an elegance it retains to this day. The brightly painted buildings, set against a backdrop of green hills, are reminiscent of those at Tobermory on the Scottish island of Mull, but the setting of Aberaeron is both unique and instantly appealing. It is without doubt one of the most cheerful and pleasant-looking

towns in Wales, much of it having evolved since the last ship was built here in 1884: thereafter the town became something of a backwater.

📷 Leave the centre of town by walking along Market Street to the main road, and there turn right to cross the bridge spanning the Afon Aeron. On the other side, go immediately left onto a surfaced pathway alongside the river, and follow this into woodland. Stay with the path until it emerges at a main road and there turn left into South Road (Stryd y Fro), and take the first turning on the right (Bro Allt-y-graig). A short way farther on, turn left into Ffordd y Goitre.

This quiet lane rises steadily, but leave it a short way after the turning to Frondeg by taking a track on the left **A**

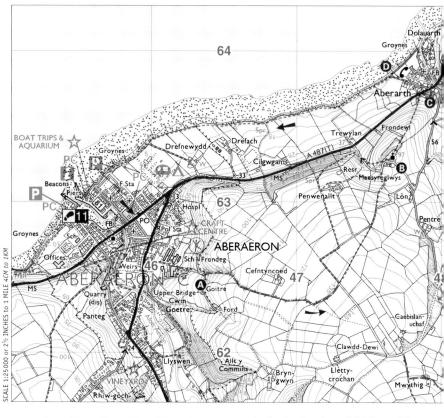

SCALE 1:25 000 or 2½ INCHES to 1 MILE 4CM to 1KM

| | 0 | 200 | 400 | 600 | 800 METRES | 1 | |
| | 0 | 200 | 400 | 600 YARDS | ½ | KILOMETRES MILES | |

leading to a gate and stile beyond which a sunken grassy track flanked by gorse rises gently. Beyond a second gate and stile the ongoing track is bordered by mature hedgerows that provide welcome shade on a hot day. Red campion, herb robert and ragwort flourish in the hedgerow which comprises mainly hawthorn, blackthorn and ivy.

When the 'covered' lane emerges at a farm access keep forward, following the track to a junction with a surfaced lane near a cattle-grid. Cross the stile opposite and keep forward along the left-hand margin of a large pasture. Continue across two more fields to reach an enclosed track that starts to descend, soon bringing St David's Church into view.

As the track swings right, leave it by going over a stile and downfield as far as a complex ladder-stile arrangement on the left. Over this, bear right, descending beside a hedgebank to another stile at the bottom of the field, giving onto a lane. Go up the lane towards the church, and, at a signpost, turn up steps and over a stone step-stile into the graveyard **B**. A church has featured on this prominent site since the 9th century, and received the attentions of marauding Vikings on more than one occasion.

Walk through the graveyard to a gate on the far side and then continue descending, with the coastal village of Aberarth now coming into view. Cross a stile in a fence corner beyond which keep forward down a trackless hill slope, initially at a gentle gradient but then with increasing steepness to a step-stile in a corner beside a garden wall. Over the stile, walk down beside the wall to a gate giving onto steps that lead down to the main road **G**.

Aberarth is a small village in a steep-sided valley, and was the harbour for this stretch of coastline before Aberaeron was built. *Taking great care against approaching traffic*, turn right and walk down towards the road bridge. Just before it, turn left on a narrow descending lane, passing houses to reach the Bethel chapel. Here keep left, briefly climbing and then following a lane between houses to a T-junction. Turn right and follow the lane down to reach the beach **D**.

Ceredigion has a 60-mile coastline, designated a Heritage Coast and dotted with small villages, ports and towns that are rich in seafaring history. The coastline between Aberarth and Aberaeron is a Site of Special Scientific Interest where bottle-nosed dolphin and Atlantic grey seal are known to feed and breed, and the sea cliffs form roosts and nest sites for nationally important populations of chough and kittiwake. The foreshore is also a fine habitat for coastal plants like scentless mayweed, hedge bindweed, hawkweed, bladder campion and ragwort.

From Aberarth go down onto the foreshore and follow the coastline back to Aberaeron. The low cliffs once carried a lovely footpath, but this has long since collapsed, necessitating a tussle with soft, grey sand and shingle. Beyond the cliffs, the path re-appears and can be followed back to Aberaeron. ●

The harbour at Aberaeron

Aberaeron to Henfynyw

		GPS waypoints
Start	Aberaeron	🔖 SN 456 630
Distance	4½ miles (7.2km)	Ⓐ SN 439 617
Approximate time	2 hours	Ⓑ SN 441 614
Parking	Aberaeron	Ⓒ SN 447 613
Refreshments	Cafés, pubs and restaurants in Aberaeron	Ⓓ SN 455 616
		Ⓔ SN 457 626
Ordnance Survey maps	Landranger 146 (Lampeter & Llandovery), Explorer 198 (Cardigan & New Quay)	

At the beginning of the 19th century, Aberaeron was a small fishing port, but after the development of the harbour its prosperity rocketed and today its wide streets and colourful terraces draw visitors from afar. The tiny village of Henfynyw, by comparison, rests its claim to fame on its association with St David, who attended a religious school here. Setting such connections aside, this walk makes the most of the spectacular coastline before turning inland to visit the church and its beautiful lychgate. The walk concludes down a leafy old green lane that leads back into Aberaeron.

🔖 Leave Aberaeron by crossing the arched footbridge spanning the Afon Aeron, and on the other side turn right along a surfaced path around the harbour. At the far side of the harbour bear left, passing a small pink building, and old weigh house, the

Sundial, St David's Church, Henfynyw

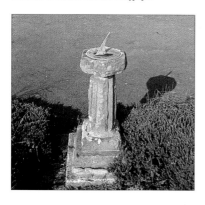

town's last reminder of the lime trade that once flourished along the Ceredigion coast.

Follow the road along the foreshore, passing the last bungalows, where the road surfacing ends, and almost immediately going left and along the right-hand edge of a large field, heading for an ornate house in the distance. The path keeps to the seaward side of the house, and starts to climb gently, flanked by low gorse bushes which thrive in this maritime climate.

Continue following the Coastal Path to another stile from which a narrow path now bears half-left uphill across the shoulder of a seaward slope to meet a fence. Follow the fence, left, to a stile in a corner. After the stile, the path begins to descend through bracken and then runs on to cross a wooded ravine by a footbridge. Keep to the right, climbing out of the ravine to continue on the Coastal Path. Eventually, the narrow path breaks free of the bracken and merges with a broader, grassy path and continues to descend.

Arrival at the deep cleft of Cwm Cilfforch 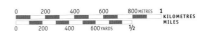 **A** is unmistakable. Through it, Ceri Brook makes a gentle approach to the sea, and needs to be crossed. Generally, this amounts to little more than a large stride or a modest leap, but occasionally, especially after heavy rain, this tiny brook may demand some intricate footwork. On the other side, climb to a stile between earth banks, and turn right alongside a fence.

Continue following the Coastal Path to another stile, from which a narrow path now bears half-left, uphill, across the shoulder of a seaward slope to meet a fence. Follow the fence, left to a stile in a field corner. Over the stile bear left onto the access to Cilcert Farm. Walk as far as a metal gate **B** at the entrance to the farm, and there drop to the left to a step-stile beside a gate. Over the stile, bear right around the edge of a rough pasture to locate another stile. Cross this and fight a way through tangled overgrowth to pop out into another pasture. Go past farm buildings to a stile in the top right-hand corner.

A lovely old green lane now awaits, flanked by mature hedgerows. Follow this as far as a stile on the left giving into an open field. Cross this obliquely right, heading down to a stile at the edge of woodland. Descend to a

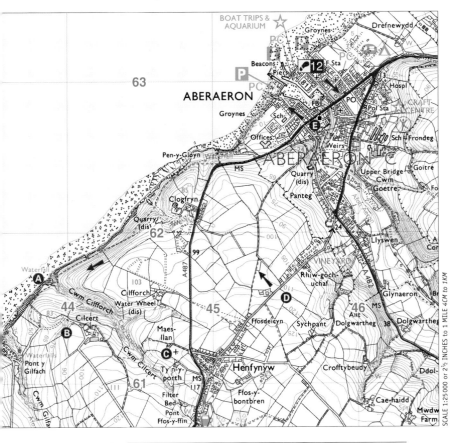

Tree-lined green lane, Henfynyw

footbridge, recrossing Ceri Brook, and, on the other side, swing left on a rising path to a stile at the top edge of the woodland in which lords and ladies grow. In the Middle Ages, this unusual flower was associated with the act of making love, and in the 16th century also had the name cuckoo pint, which some think is a corruption of 'cuckold' – a man whose wife has been unfaithful. The roots of lords and ladies produced a high starch content which in Tudor times was used to stiffen the high, pleated ruffs that were fashionable. *Please note: the berries are poisonous, and can be fatal.*

From the top edge of the woodland, an enclosed path leads around a large pasture to a greystone house, Maes-y-Llan **C**. Walk out along the house driveway and follow it to the entrance to St David's Church. The lychgate is a fine example, in front of which stands a sundial.

Cross the busy road in front of the church and walk along the lane opposite. At the next junction turn left and continue down the lane as far as a stile on the left **D**, after a farm and just before a row of houses begins. Leave the road and walk along the right-hand hedgebank and, on the far side of the field, bear right onto a broad track enclosed between fences, later becoming a stony track between mature hedgerows. This is a lovely old lane that descends steadily towards Aberaeron.

The lane eventually emerges at a main road, opposite the Pencarreg Craft Centre **E**. Cross the road, and go into the lane opposite, immediately bearing right on a signposted path, but a few strides farther on, as the path swings right, leaving it by continuing forward down a leafy path that descends quite steeply to a surfaced path beside the Afon Aeron.

Turn left and follow the river back to the road bridge at Aberaeron and the conclusion of the walk. ●

Plynlimon

		GPS waypoints
Start	Eisteddfa Gurig	⬛ SN 798 841
Distance	5 miles (8km)	**A** SN 796 858
Approximate time	3 hours	**B** SN 797 841
Parking	Eisteddfa Gurig (charge)	**C** SN 786 841
Refreshments	Dyffryn Castell and Ponterwyd	
Ordnance Survey maps	Landranger 135 (Aberystwyth & Machynlleth), Explorer 213 (Aberystwyth & Cwm Rheidol)	

The ascent to the highest summit in Ceredigion is, as mountains go, comparatively straightforward and thoroughly enjoyable, but it is not an outing for anything other than a clear day of settled weather: *getting down is easy enough, but* finding the top in poor visibility could become a very hit-and-miss affair and some map and compass work may be required. *On a good day the view is outstanding and the sense of being far away from anything heightened by the passage of red kites and buzzards that vie for airspace with ravens.*

For centuries the extensive boglands of Plynlimon, or Pumlumon Fawr in Welsh, separated north and south Wales; they also supplied the wherewithal for five rivers, the Dulas and the Clywedog to the north-east, the Rheidol on the north-west, the Wye (which rises only a short distance from the summit of the mountain), and the longest river in Britain, the Severn. At the foot of the mountain, near Ponterwyd, lies one of the main centres of the silver and lead mining industry in Wales: there were more than 90 pits in northern Ceredigion alone. Innocuous the mountain may seem – although getting a clear view of it is not easy: the shores of Nant-y-moch Reservoir being the best place – but it holds a significance far greater than its huge, boggy bulk.

Black's *Picturesque Guide to North Wales* describes Plinlimmon (sic) as 'the most dangerous mountain in Wales', owing to the 'frequency of bogs, concealed under a smooth and apparently firm turf.' It goes on to express the view that 'few travellers who make the ascent deem themselves recompensed for the toil and hazard.' This was a view shared by the Reverend W Bingley, who wrote: 'From the various accounts that had reached me respecting this mountain, there did not appear any probable compensation for my trouble in going so far out of my road to ascend its summit, I therefore continued my route and only passed it at a distance.'

Plynlimon, in its widest sense, consists of a vast group of mountains of which three in particular are pre-eminent. On these three are piles of stone, principally five in number, hence 'Pumlumon', Five Stacks, commonly alleged to cover the remains of warriors slain in battle and serving as memorials

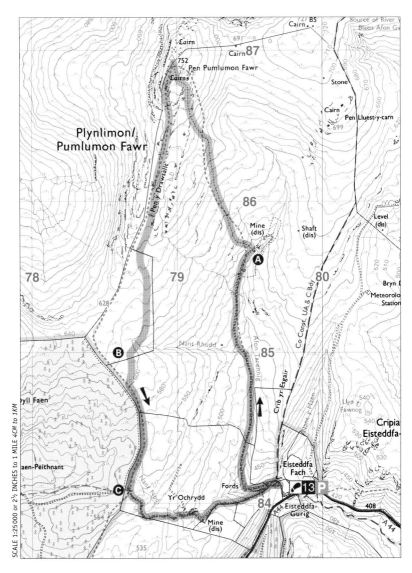

SCALE 1:25000 or 2½ INCHES to 1 MILE 4CM to 1KM

| 0 | 200 | 400 | 600 | 800 METRES | 1 |
| 0 | 200 | 400 | 600 YARDS | ½ | |

KILOMETRES
MILES

to their exploits.

🖊 The walk begins at a private parking area adjoining the farmhouse at Eisteddfa Gurig. Walk back out to the road and turn right, walking the short distance to a signposted bridleway on the right, heading through two metal gates, and then going forward along a farm track to another gate with a sign 'All Walks'. Beyond the gate, the track

swings round to follow the course of the Afon Tarennig, and climbs steadily. After a gate, the track levels and starts to descend for a short while, climbing again as it heads up towards old mine workings. Here, at a waymark post Ⓐ, branch left onto a stony path that suddenly comes to an end.

A generally clear grassy path now takes the route on, teasing a way upwards, and, higher up, meeting a more pronounced and cairned path that guides the route onto the surprisingly rocky top of the mountain, marked by a trig pillar and a shelter. A ladder-stile across a fence gives access to the summit.

From the summit, the view northwards embraces Cadair Idris and the Arans, swinging eastwards to take in the Berwyn Hills and the Border Marches, and south to the Brecon Beacons, with Pen y Fan, Corn Du, Bannau Brycheiniog and Bannau Sir Gaer all distinguishable along the far horizon.

The summit fence is the key to the surest way down in mist. Go back to the ladder-stile and over it turn right alongside the fence. Initially the path is not all that distinct, but then one appears, and crosses a low ridge, Pen y Drawsallt, continuing downwards easily to meet a section of moorland temporarily fenced for conservation purposes. *In poor visibility it is best to stick with the fence on leaving the summit, as far as the enclosed area.*

Cross a step-stile into the enclosed area, and generally parallel the left-hand fenceline; there is a basic path most of the way, but a few stretches where there is none. By sticking with the left-hand fenceline, you eventually come to a metal gate at the head of a broad track. A step-stile **B** a short distance to the right gets you over the fence, and onto a short path that leads out to meet the track at a signpost.

Turn right and follow the broad track as it descends through a gate (stile nearby), and keep on until it meets a cross-path **C** emerging from a plantation on the right. Here, swing left and follow a broad track all the way down to Eisteddfa Gurig, retracing your steps at the farm to go out through the two gates, onto the road, and turning left to the car park.   ●

On the summit of Plynlimon looking towards Nant-y-moch Reservoir

Strata Florida

Start	Strata Florida	GPS waypoints
Distance	5 miles (8km)	⌁ SN 746 657
Approximate time	2½ hours	Ⓐ SN 728 661
Parking	Strata Florida	Ⓑ SN 730 650
Refreshments	Pontrhydfendigaid	Ⓒ SN 738 642
Ordnance Survey maps	Landranger 147 (Elan Valley & Builth Wells), Explorer 187 (Llandovery)	Ⓓ SN 745 649

Exploring the countryside that once fell under the influence of the pastoral Cistercian monks at Strata Florida, this walk loses itself among the pastoral folds and old green lanes south of the Vale of Flowers before ambling back along forest trails and bridleways. Allow time to explore the abbey remains and the churchyard alongside, which contains the now seriously cropped yew tree that marks the site of the grave of Dafydd ap Gwilym, Wales' greatest medieval poet. There is a marked serenity about this verdant corner of Ceredigion that is almost tangible.

The abbey at Strata Florida was founded by Robert Fitzstephen in the 12th century and grew to become the richest and most influential centre of Welsh culture – it has been described as the Westminster of Wales – a place patronised by princes and poets alike, the depository of Welsh national records, and with a potent voice in Welsh politics. The Order was Cistercian, traced to the foundation of the 'New Monastery' at Citeaux in Burgundy and renowned for seeking out wild and lonely places, not only to enhance the spirit of remoteness but also to enable the monks to pursue sheep farming, something they did with great skill and determination. The monks, who came from Whitland Abbey, managed large estates, clearing the original woodlands to provide pasturage for their sheep and cattle. Around Strata Florida there were

originally five large farms, called 'granges', although this eventually grew to 15 in number. Although now in ruins, Strata Florida still displays evidence of its former importance, and many Welsh princes are believed to be buried here. In 1284, King Edward I destroyed the abbey in revenge against Prince Madoc for taking part in a local rebellion. More than a century later, Henry IV used the ruined abbey as a base from which to pursue Owain Glyndwr.

⌁ Set off over a stile just into the lane past the telephone box, and cross to a footbridge. On the other side, head across to another stile after which a narrow grassy path accompanies the river at varying distances. Throughout its trek across fields, the path is clear, waymarked and stiled, leading eventually to a farm access. Turn left and walk out past the Black Lion Hotel

to meet the B4348 road through
Pontrhydfendigaid, the Bridge of the
Blessed Ford.

Continue up the road for 660 yds
(600m) to a stile on the left at the edge
of the Bryn y Gors Holiday Park **A**.
Cross the stile and walk down a wide
grassy track to enter the caravan site.
Go into the site and continue down its
left-hand edge to a step-stile in a field
corner *(or to avoid invading people's
privacy, use the caravan site road to the
far side and, as it bends right, leave it*

*and go left after the last caravan to
the corner stile).* Over the stile, keep
forward in the same direction to a metal
gate. Now go forward moving slightly
away from the left-hand fence to a gate
gap about 45 yds (40m) to the right of
a ruin.

From the gap, keep on in the same
direction, now climbing across rough
pasture aiming for the right-hand edge

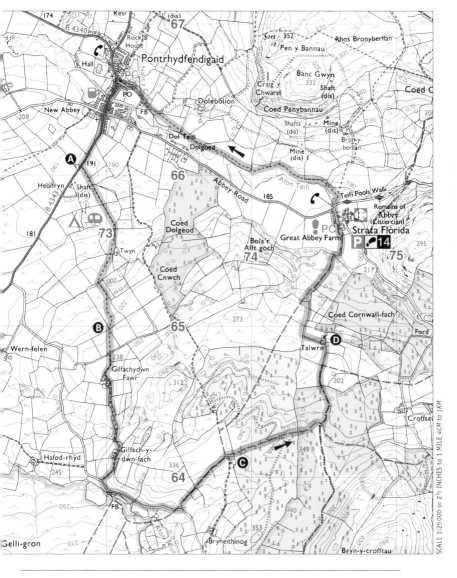

SCALE 1:25000 or 2½ INCHES to 1 MILE 4CM to 1KM

of a small woodland to locate a step-stile in a fence corner. Cross the stile and initially go forward alongside a fence, about as far as a metal gate on the left, and then cut diagonally up to the top corner of the field where a step-stile gives onto a metal gate. There is no clear path on this section and an intermediate fence, partially concealed, makes it difficult to take a precise line: the top right-hand corner of the field is the target **B**.

Through the metal gate, head obliquely up to an open barn and another gate. Then go forward along an access track to Gilfachydwn Fawr Farm. Keep to the left of the farm to reach a gate and small barn-like building beyond. Go to the left of the building and a short way farther on, where the track indistinctly forks, branch right on the lower of two paths, an old green lane that leads to a gate giving into light woodland.

Keep on in the same direction, along the top edge of the woodland, to reach Gilfach-y-dwn-fach Farm, passing it on the right and then walk out along its access to a lane. Turn left and follow the lane past an obsolete building, to a gate where the road surfacing ends. A rough track continues beyond: take this as far as the second metal gate on the left, from which a clear vehicle track strikes up the left-hand edge of a field. Walk up the track towards a barn, and just before reaching it, go left through a gate and then immediately right to a wooden gate giving into a plantation **C**.

Walk through a break in the plantation to meet a forest trail. Bear right, and shortly, when the trail bends right, leave it by keeping forward through another forest break. Pass through a fence and keep on in the same direction with the path seasonally overgrown by bracken, and now descending. Lower down, the path merges with an indistinct grassy track, which bears left and continues descending to a small metal gate at which it leaves the plantation. Keep forward along a lovely old green lane which comes down to the ruined cottages at Talwrn **D**.

Walk in front of the first cottage to locate another green lane. Follow this to its end at a gate and through this turn right down the edge of a field, parallel with a stream and later a fence that curves round to a metal gate. Go through the gate onto an indistinct descending bridleway that goes into light woodland where the path becomes clearer and later descends parallel with a low, moss-covered wall. It then goes down to a footbridge and stile at which the woodland cover is left for a wide track going forward beside a wall. This leads down to the road at Strata Florida, emerging next to the entrance to the car park. ●

The ruined farm at Talwrn

Penbryn

		GPS waypoints	
Start	Penbryn (Llanborth)	 SN 296 522	
Distance	5½ miles (8.8km)	Ⓐ SN 297 528	
Approximate time	3 hours	Ⓑ SN 309 542	
Parking	National Trust car park, Penbryn (Pay and Display)	Ⓒ SN 311 534	
		Ⓓ SN 314 526	
Refreshments	Café at Penbryn, pubs and cafés at Llangranog	Ⓔ SN 305 521	
Ordnance Survey maps	Landranger 145 (Cardigan & Mynydd Preseli), Explorer 198 (Cardigan & New Quay)		

Penbryn has a beach quite disproportionate to the size of this farming hamlet, but this walk concentrates on beaches only when viewed from above. Beginning with a stretch of the coastline leading to the adjacent village of Llangrannog, the route then wanders inland to explore the wooded Hoffnant Valley before returning through the shaded broad-leaved confines of Troed y Rhiw. The clifftop section is quite a switchback and steep in places, but is well-waymarked and nowhere difficult.

From the Llanborth car park at Penbryn, turn immediately left onto a track beside a farm, signposted for Llangrannog. Pass through a metal gate and onto a track rising between hedgebanks. At a signpost keep left, still climbing, and follow the rising track as far as a signposted path on the left. Here, go through a wooden kissing-gate Ⓐ to begin a spectacular cliff top passage to Llangrannog. From a stile, soon encountered, the on-going path is well waymarked as it roller-coasters northwards. It descends steeply to cross an in-flowing stream below the hill fort remains of Castell Bach. Steep steps take the path upwards from the stream to a stile and a brief enclosed path, after which it

continues its upwards march through gorse and other prickly shrubs. This leads to an enclosed clifftop path that later breaks free again as it begins its descent towards Llangrannog.

The path eventually comes down to

The coastline between Penbryn and Llangrannog

SCALE 1:25000 or 2½ INCHES to 1 MILE 4CM to 1KM

0	200	400	600	800 METRES	1
					KILOMETRES
					MILES
0	200	400	600 YARDS		½

the top end of a surfaced lane **B**. Turn right onto this and go down to Llangrannog passing an old lime kiln.

On reaching the beach front in Llangrannog, turn right up a lane climbing past the Pentre Arms. Follow this as it twists upwards and ignore a branching road on the left. When the road surfacing ends, keep forward past houses onto a narrow path through bracken and blackthorn, ascending gently onto the hillside south of Llangrannog. Climb to a metal kissing-

gate beyond which the path continues through another gate and up to a step-stile giving onto a farm track **C**. Go ahead onto this and up to a T-junction near Eisteddfa Farm. Turn right and in the farmyard bear left to walk past the farmhouse and follow the access out to meet a lane.

Turn right and, *taking care against traffic*, follow the lane for 440 yds (400m) and then leave it by turning left onto a signposted path along a broad, hedgerowed track **D**. After a gentle climb, the track arrives at a point overlooking the lovely, wooded Hoffnant Valley. The track now briefly

48 ● WALK 15

zigzags down and then forks. Take the left branch, continuing down a vehicle track to meet a narrow lane. Turn sharp right and follow this pleasant lane for almost a mile (1.4km) to a T-junction. Turn right and walk up an adjoining lane as far as a signposted path on the left for Llangrannog and Penbryn **E**. Just above this point stands the Pen Morfa Chapel.

Leave the road at a signpost and go forward a short distance into a sloping pasture to locate a path branching left, into light woodland and descending to intercept a horizontal path lower down. This leads, right, to a metal gate and into the leafy shade of Troed y Rhiw. The path emerges onto a rising access track to an isolated house. Go past the house and through a wooden gate onto a descending grassy track that soon meets the stony track used at the start of the walk. Turn left to go back down to Penbryn, and so conclude the walk. ●

On the Coastal Path above Llangrannog

Devil's Bridge and the Mynach Valley

Start	Devil's Bridge
Distance	5½ miles (8.8km)
Approximate time	2½–3 hours
Parking	Devil's Bridge
Refreshments	Cafés at Devil's Bridge
Ordnance Survey maps	Landranger 135 (Aberystwyth & Machynlleth), Explorer 213 (Aberystwyth & Cwm Rheidol)

GPS waypoints

- ✏ SN 739 769
- Ⓐ SN 749 765
- Ⓑ SN 748 771
- Ⓒ SN 761 772
- Ⓓ SN 770 779
- Ⓔ SN 771 776

The beauty of the Mynach Valley is unsurpassed in Mid Wales, and this walk lets visitors take in the scenery from both sides of the valley as well as from an elevated position above it. A good way to reach Devil's Bridge is by railway from Aberystwyth, which adds another satisfying element to the walk. Long stretches of the walk are over rough terrain and rutted paths, so strong footwear is essential.

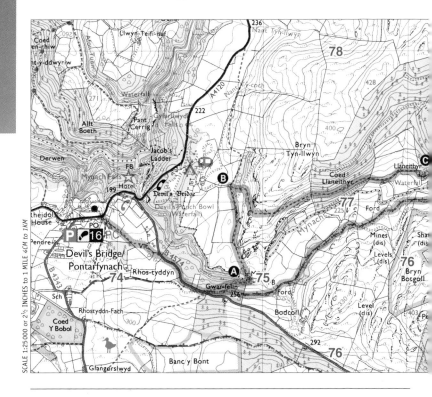

✏️ Leave Devil's Bridge by walking up the lane opposite the railway car park, and go through a gate and along an enclosed path to the left of the toilets. When the path opens into a field, head across this towards the left-hand edge of a small plantation, and then bear left across rough ground to locate a gate at the back of a house garden. Turn right along the boundary fence to find a step-stile over a fence, from which head slightly left to another stile giving onto the B4574. Turn right and follow the road for about 440 yds (400m), and then leave it by branching left on a signposted bridleway for Aber Bodcoll. Almost immediately, leave the access track for a footpath descending left and shortly running into light woodland.

Here, at the site of the old Bodcoll Mill **A**, cross a footbridge spanning the Afon Mynach and bear left on a

Beside the Mynach

waymarked path, climbing to a stile at the top edge of the woodland. Keep climbing and go round the end of two rocky hillocks on the right to locate a stile to the right of a metal gate. Over this, turn left along a broad grassy track. Continue as far as a waymark on the right **B**, here leaving the track and climbing a slope in the shade of oak trees to intercept a field track. Cross this to another waymark at the foot of a bracken-covered slope and at the edge of a small spread of oak trees. At the waymark, bear right, along an initially indistinct path which soon starts to rise through bracken to another waymark where the path turns left, across, but not significantly up, a grassy slope to another waymark and a lovely view up the valley.

The path now descends through dense bracken and then gorse to a step-stile. Over this, cross a small stream and keep forward into a pine plantation through which a gentle path leads into shade where wood sorrel and star moss grow in abundance. When the path emerges from the plantation, go down to run along a broad track. Follow this to pass Llaneithyr **C**, beyond which the

In the Mynach Valley

track runs on towards a gate, following which it forks. Branch right on a gently descending track along the base of a mature plantation.

For a while the track is accompanied on the right by a large open expanse. Just as this starts to come to an end, leave the ongoing track at a waymark on the right, and go down steps to cross the Afon Merin by a footbridge **D**, and then enter the cleared area, climbing on an indistinct grassy path to intercept an old grassy road at a waymark. The old road bears right to a ford near the confluence of the Afon Merin and the Nant Rhuddnant, which from here on form the Afon Mynach. The ford, however, is not passable by pedestrians, but there is a footbridge upstream. From the waymark where the old road was first reached, head for the footbridge **E**, although it is initially unseen.

This part of the valley is extremely beautiful, green and lush and peaceful. Overhead buzzards have given way to red kites and the occasional foraying

goshawk. Over the bridge, turn right across a stile and follow a riverside path. *For a while the ongoing riverside path is deeply rutted, boggy and partially overgrown, making progress both slow and potentially hazardous for anyone not wearing appropriate footwear.* After a couple of metal gates in quick succession the ongoing track moves away from the river as it rolls across sheep pastures. A slight pull up to a wooden gate, where there is one last chance to take in the retrospective view up this delightful valley, and then the ongoing track significantly improves. When it forks, branch right through a metal gate and soon enter an old green lane that leads down to a step-stile with a footbridge beyond, giving onto a grassy path leading to the cottage at Aber Bodcoll.

Go past the cottage and keep forward on its stony access lane, which leads out to rejoin the outward track at the B-road. Turn right, and retrace the outward route to Devil's Bridge. ●

Soar y Mynydd and the Afon Doethie

		GPS waypoints	
Start	Soar y Mynydd		SN 784 534
Distance	6 miles (9.6km)	**A**	SN 789 526
Approximate time	3 hours	**B**	SN 771 514
Parking	Soar y Mynydd	**C**	SN 757 734
Refreshments	None		
Ordnance Survey maps	Landranger 147 (Elan Valley & Builth Wells), Explorer 187 (Llandovery)		

The sound of silence is a most agreeable companion on this simple and exquisite exploration of the moorlands that fringe the border between Ceredigion and Powys: red kite country for sure, but a place where solitude is supplied in abundance. Few people are likely to be able to pinpoint the Doethie valley with certainty, but its sudden revelation as the walk progresses is truly breathtaking, a steep-sided gorge of great beauty insinuated between voluptuous folds of lush green hills. Of course, this is a remote walk, and anyone tackling it needs to be well stocked with provisions, suitable equipment and clothing.

There is parking near the Soar y Mynydd Chapel, or beside a roadside Jubilee Stone placed in 1977 to commemorate the planting of the surrounding forest in 1952. From the stone take the track down, crossing the Camddwr, to the white-painted chapel, which is accessed by an attractive wooden footbridge built, it is said, to honour a custom in the bride's country when a local lad married a Malaysian girl.

The chapel has its foundations in services first held in 1740 at Rhiwalog Farm, which were popular because not only did they afford the local people a chance to worship in Welsh, but also gave them the opportunity, to meet up with friends and neighbours. The chapel was built in 1822 on land donated by Nantllwyd Farm, and is still regarded as the most remote chapel in Wales. By 1960 the congregation had dwindled almost to single figures, but then saw

Green lane in Nant Doethie

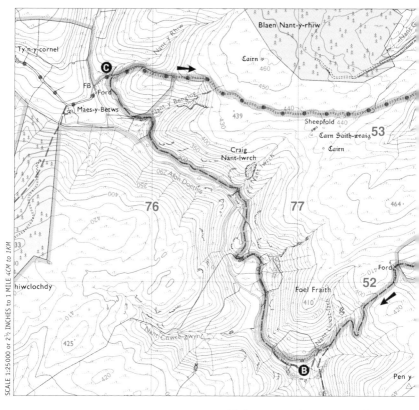

quite a revival. Today, it remains a beautiful chapel, and, on the last Sunday in August, holds a special service that fills the church to over-flowing.

🥾 Walk past the chapel and cross a cattle-grid, going forward on a gently rising track. Follow this for about ½ mile (800m) until, as the track bends right, a branching path leads right, to a metal gate **A**. Through the gate continue along the track to reach Nantllwyd Farm. Go past the first farm building, and then follow waymarks to a metal gate giving into a sloping paddock. Turn left, following a track to a higher gate which gives onto moorland pasture.

The small valley of Nant-llwyd once held up to 28 small farms, many built under 15th-century legislation which enabled a man to claim an area of common land for himself if, within a day, he could build a basic house – four walls and a chimney – and have a fire burning in the grate, within 24 hours. Such buildings, although there are none now in Nant-llwyd, are easy to identify because they tended to have rather over-large chimneys which were built like that so that they could support the weight of the rest of the house, which didn't need to be quite so substantial, in order to comply with the law.

Beyond the farm, continue on a gated track into red kite country, where the successful efforts to reintroduce the species to Wales began. Eventually, the track ends and the route continues as a narrow footpath across a grassy col between low hills. As the path starts to descend, suddenly the beauty of the Doethie valley springs into view, a breathtaking moment. A green path snakes down to cross the Nant Lluest-fach,

to turn into the upper part of the Doethie valley. The path wanders easily up the valley and, as it draws level with more ruins, turn initially towards them, but within a few strides bear right, climbing along the edge of more bracken on an improving path that crosses a hill shoulder.

Once beyond the in-flowing Nant Iwrch the path presses on delightfully, passing more ruins and soon meeting a bridlegate. Beyond this it gradually bends right to another gate giving onto a broad stony track **C**. Turn right onto this, climbing steadily onto the moors above with fine views of distant mountains and the nearby rippling folds of the Doethie and its feeder streams. The track is one of the old drove roads of Wales from Llanddewibrefi, heading into England, and along which, 200 years ago, herds of Welsh black cattle and flocks of sheep would have been encountered.

continuing then as a stony path through bracken and seasonally overgrown. Just after a ruined building **B**, bear right through more dense stands of bracken

The track climbs onto bleak moorland where it levels, before another short climb takes it up to its highest point before a long descent leads back to the Soar y Mynydd Chapel and the conclusion of the walk.　　　●

Soar y Mynydd Chapel

Llanerchaeron

		GPS waypoints
Start	Aberaeron	SN 456 630
Distance	5¾ miles (9.2km)	**A** SN 465 616
Approximate time	2–2½ hours	**B** SN 477 605
Parking	Aberaeron	**C** SN 478 603
Refreshments	Cafés, pubs and restaurants in Aberaeron	
Ordnance Survey maps	Landranger 146 (Lampeter & Llandovery), Explorer 198 (Cardigan & New Quay)	

This mainly wooded walk follows the Afon Aeron up-river to the lovely Church of St Non and then to the National Trust's Llanerchaeron Estate, one of the few remaining properties in this part of Wales that were built for the landed gentry. The return simply follows the track-bed of an old railway, which makes for easy walking. Throughout the walk there is an abundance of woodland birdlife and in spring and early summer a host of wild flowers to brighten the way.

Leave Aberaeron along Market Street to the main road, and turn right to cross the bridge over the Afon Aeron. Go immediately left onto a surfaced pathway alongside the river, and follow this into woodland. Stay with the path until it emerges at a main road and there turn left into South Road (Stryd y Fro), and take the first turning on the right (Bro Allt-y-graig). Follow the ascending road past the turning into Ffordd y Goitre, and keep forward until the lane bends right at Allt y Gog. Leave it by branching left onto a track rising into the Allt y Graig woodland, which is a typical example of an oak and ash woodland and, like many of the forests in this part of Wales, clear-felled during the Second World War. Little is known about the management of the woodland although some areas of the estate do appear as wooded on a 19th-century Ordnance Survey map.

At a wooden gate turn immediately left, climbing on a broad path, and, at a fenced area, passing above a small quarry that was used to provide building materials for prominent public and domestic buildings in Aberaeron. Eventually, the path turns right and descends steeply in places. At a lower path, where the descending route forks, branch left at a yellow waymark, continuing steeply down steps to meet a surfaced lane. Turn left.

At College Farm **A**, where the road surfacing ends, keep forward, once more entering woodland and following a broad path. The path descends to almost touch on the track-bed of an old railway that will be used for the return part of the walk. Here, keep forward and go over a stile beside a metal gate, continuing along the bottom edge of woodland to reach the edge of a large clearing. Immediately, bear right along a path enfolded within overhanging trees which parallels the bottom edge of the clearing before moving away as it runs between low moss-covered walls. Shortly, pass a derelict building, just after which a step-stile takes the route on, along the top edge of a steep wooded bank to another stile beyond which a small stream is crossed.

In the ensuing pasture follow the left boundary to a gap in a corner. Keep forward along the left edge of the next field to reach a farm access. Cross a stile and turn left for a few strides, then bear right over another stile and along a rough track. Continue past another derelict building and maintain the same direction on another lovely wooded walk and eventually crossing the Afon Aeron at a footbridge **B**.

Cross a narrow field to a gate giving

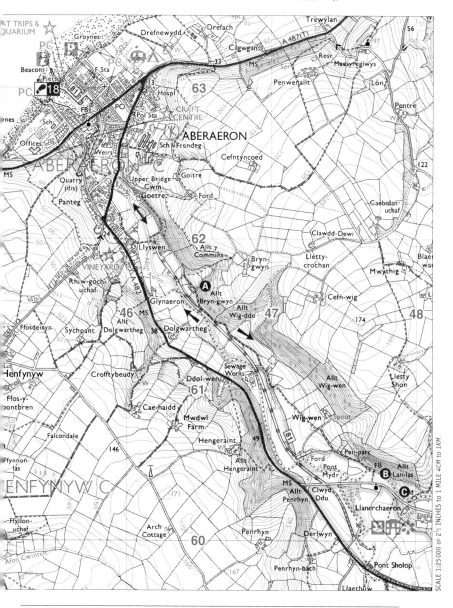

The Regency house at Llanerchaeron

onto a lane. Turn left to St Non's Church wherein lie a number of seafaring people and one unfortunate soldier. Go past the church to reach the entrance to Llanerchaeron. This is a traditional rural estate, maintained in the same family for ten generations, and still complete with its Regency house, designed by the famous architect John Nash, servants' quarters, stables, farm buildings and walled garden. In the late 18th century, Llanerchaeron was very much at the forefront of agricultural development in Wales and, in addition to meeting all its own needs, also played a part in the local community. The estate is now in the care of the National Trust, who, commendably, still manage it as a working organic farm: the two walled gardens producing home-grown vegetables and flowers. The house is open daily (except Mondays and Tuesdays) from March until November.

Go back along the road from the entrance to Llanerchaeron, and leave the road just after a set of gates on the left by turning left at a footpath sign **ⓒ**. From a kissing-gate strike across a large pasture aiming for a white-topped pole in the middle distance, and from this bear left to locate a gate in the fence boundary giving onto a footbridge spanning the Afon Mydr.

Over the bridge, turn left onto a track for a few strides, and then turn right onto an old railway track-bed, a thoroughfare flanked by mature ash, birch and sycamore as well as the usual scrubby undergrowth that grows up along disused railway lines. The track soon leads out to a road. Cross, and continue in the same direction. Soon recross the Afon Aeron, and keep forward through a gate onto the continuing track, now enclosed between fences.

The ongoing track eventually emerges into a small parking area. Go across this to a T-junction and there turn left on a surfaced lane that becomes Bro Allt-y-graig. At the main road turn left and cross the road bridge, going right on the other side to follow the riverside path back into Aberaeron. ●

Aberystwyth to Clarach Bay

		GPS waypoints
Start	Aberystwyth	SN 581 818
Distance	6¼ miles (10km)	Ⓐ SN 594 837
Approximate time	3 hours	Ⓑ SN 617 838
Parking	Aberystwyth	Ⓒ SN 602 832
Refreshments	Cafés, pubs and restaurants in Aberystwyth	Ⓓ SN 596 829
Ordnance Survey maps	Landranger 135 (Aberystwyth & Machynlleth), Explorer 213 (Aberystwyth & Cwm Rheidol)	

A short, sharp climb leads to a fine, airy traverse above Cardigan Bay to Clarach Bay, a place of neatly regimented caravans and static homes from where the walk turns inland. This provides a complete contrast by following the edge of farm fields along the course of the Afon Clarach before making a fine cross-country return using old tracks, woodland paths and the edge of a golf course. Views seaward are good, but those inland to the hills of central Wales are especially inspiring.

Begin by walking northwards along the promenade in Aberystwyth and, at its far end, turn right and climb a flight of concrete steps that leads to the lower station of the cliff railway. Near the top of the steps, turn left on a signposted path for Constitution Hill (Y Graig Glais).

Keep following the main ascending path, which climbs steeply in zigzags and twice crosses the cliff railway, but finally hauls up onto a small plateau from where another path is signposted for Clarach. Keep forward along this; it runs along a steep cliff slope before descending along the edge of a small plantation to overlook Clarach Bay, where rows of static caravans and wooden chalets fill the valley sides.

The path eventually descends to meet a narrow road. Bear right along this until a side road joins from the right Ⓐ, and there leave the road by branching left onto a signposted footpath

descending gently through roadside scrub to the edge of an estate of wooden chalets. Turn right through the top edge of the site, locating a path that runs at the back of the chalets to a step-stile in a corner at the far end of the site.

Over the stile, strike across a large pasture, roughly aiming for Ffynnon Ddu, and locate another stile tucked into a hedgerow, close by an overhead powerline pole. Cross the next field, aiming for a waymarked gate near Ffynnon Ddu, and turn right through the gate onto a surfaced access lane.

The lane leads down to a road at Llangorwen, where a short diversion, left, to visit All Saints Church is worthwhile (although the church is usually locked). Otherwise, cross the road and pass to the right of a cottage at the back of which a step-stile gives into another field.

Go forward along the bottom edge of the field, parallel with the Afon Clarach,

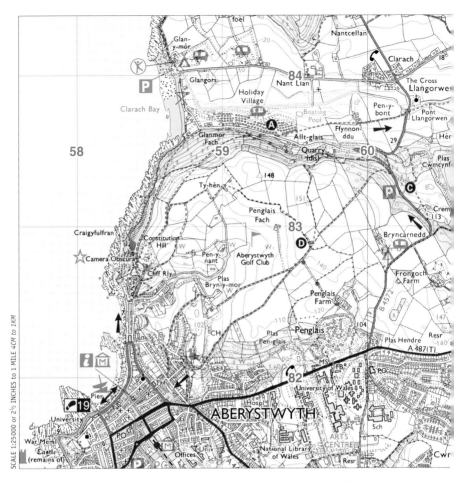

SCALE 1:25000 or 2½ INCHES to 1 MILE 4CM to 1KM

```
0    200   400   600   800 METRES   1
                                        KILOMETRES
                                        MILES
0    200   400   600 YARDS    ½
```

heading for a field corner stile beside a gate. The path, barely noticeable on the ground, now follows the margins of a series of fields bordered by high stands of gorse, and crossing into the ensuing fields either at gates or stiles before finally locating an overgrown step-stile in a field corner, which gives onto a rough track **B**.

Turn right to a gate and follow the track towards Rhyd-tir Isaf Farm, but after only a few strides leave it by branching left onto a rutted track climbing towards the woodland of Coed Rhyd-tir. The track soon bears right and starts to climb between gorse and bracken.

The ascending track forks near a gate. Here, bear right, through the gate, and a few strides farther on, when the main track swings left into a pasture, leave it, on the apex of the bend, going forward on a grassy path which climbs gently with improving views northwards, and soon runs along the top edge of a small broad-leaved woodland, and continues beyond as a clear, old track flanked by ash, rowan, blackthorn and hawthorn.

Through a metal gate keep forward along the right-hand field boundary, where the old trackway is sunken and partially overgrown by hawthorn. It descends steadily to another gate beyond which it continues to follow the field boundary to emerge at a surfaced lane.

Turn onto the lane, which climbs to a junction with a main road. Turn right

Clarach Bay

here, and, *taking great care against approaching traffic*, follow the road as far as a lay-by on the left, just as the road bends to the right **C**.

At the lay-by take the left-hand one of two flights of steps and climb into beech woodland. Towards the top edge of the woodland, bear right across a footbridge, and then follow the footpath along the woodland boundary. When the boundary path changes direction, turn left with it and walk gently uphill to a gate and stile at the top edge of the woodland. Over this, go forward along the left-hand margin of the next field.

At the next field corner, cross a stile, maintaining the same direction but now having switched sides of the on-going field boundary. From the next stile, strike out across a meadow to a stile on the opposite side, giving onto an enclosed track alongside a golf course **D**.

Ignore the first turning on the left (a broad track), but a short way farther on, turn left through a wooden kissing-gate onto a path enclosed between hedgerows. Keep following the path, which eventually emerges onto a woodland path. This is initially level but then starts to descend through the Parc Natur Penglais. The park, which largely embraces a fine deciduous woodland and was once part of the Plas Penglais Estate, offers fine view across Cardigan Bay, Aberystwyth, Pendinas and the lower Rheidol Valley. The path emerges into gorse directly above Aberystwyth, which has now appeared below, and finally runs out to meet a road at a bend.

Follow the road as it zigzags down to a T-junction. There turn right, and immediately left into Loveden Road and, at the bottom, turn right into Queen's Road and left along Portland Street at the end of which the promenade is only a short distance off to the right. ●

Trefechan to Morfa Bychan

		GPS waypoints
Start	Trefechan beach	
Distance	6⅓ miles (10.2km)	✒ SN 579 807
Approximate time	3 hours	**A** SN 576 790
Parking	Trefechan beach	**B** SN 570 777
Refreshments	Trefechan and Aberystwyth	**C** SN 568 771
Ordnance Survey maps	Landranger 135 (Aberystwyth & Machynlleth), Explorer 213 (Aberystwyth & Cwm Rheidol)	**D** SN 571 773
		E SN 575 774
		F SN 583 784

Viewed from the pebbly beach at Trefechan, the sharp profile of Allt Wen to the south seems only to promise hard work. So it will come as an agreeable surprise to discover that once this shapely height has been conquered all that remains until you reach Morfa Bychan is a delightful and gently undulating stroll high above the waves. Although much of the return is along hedgerowed lanes, these usually have only light traffic, and in spring and early summer are bright with wild flowers. Keep an eye open over the adjacent fields for visiting red kite.

✒ Start from the foreshore parking space and set off south along a broad track in the lee of the breakwater. On the far side of the bay, follow the signposted Coastal Path, which climbs steeply for a while above Allt Wen.

When you reach a gate **A**, the worst of the ascent is over, and the ongoing path continues at a much easier gradient.

The clifftop path is accompanied by a fence, and eventually arrives at a couple of adjacent stiles in a corner. Cross both, and continue on the seaward side of a fence. This is a delightful stretch. Eventually, the path descends as Morfa Bychan, identified by its caravan site, comes into view. Cross a stile/gate and continue descending to pass around a wide dry cove **B**, after which you bear left alongside a fence to another stile one field away from the caravan site.

Set off towards the caravan site, but half-way across the field bear left,

uphill, towards a waymark, and then climb to a stile in a fence above. Over the stile, go forward on a grassy path through a short stretch of bracken; there is a dilapidated wall on your right, buried beneath the bracken and scrub, so it is not obvious. But follow this wall, climbing gently, to meet another at right angles. Where the walls meet, go forward to a signpost a short distance farther on, and from it take to a grassy track through gorse that leads out to meet a minor road at a stile and gate **C**. Turn left and walk up the road, crossing a cattle-grid along the way.

As the road bends to the right, leave it by going forward over a stile **D**. In the ensuing pasture, keep ahead, below a spread of gorse on your left, and at the top of the field, head for a stile. Over the stile, bear right towards a low wall impregnated with wind-blown hawthorns. Pass around the end of the

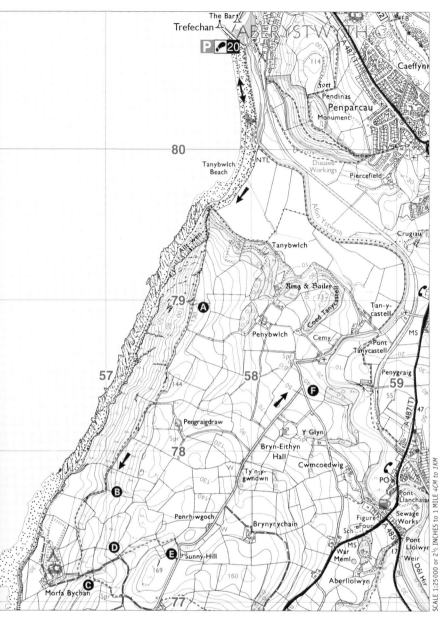

wall, and then follow it to a step-stile in a corner giving onto a narrow lane **E**.

Turn left and follow the lane for a little over a mile (2km), descending eventually to a T-junction **F**. Go left again, and follow the descending road to pass a church. A short way farther on you reach a bridge (Pont Tan y Castell) spanning the Afon Ystwyth.

Do not cross the bridge, but leave the road by passing through a metal

kissing-gate on the left, beside the river, to gain a broad riverside track. The track now accompanies the river back to the shore. Stay with it as the river bends to the right, and take to a narrow path slightly lower than your outward route at this point to conclude the walk.

Trefeurig

Trefeurig

		GPS waypoints
Start	Llyn Pendam, above Cwmsymlog	📖 SN 711 839
Distance	6¼ miles (10km)	Ⓐ SN 700 838
Approximate time	3 hours	Ⓑ SN 690 843
Parking	Llyn Pendam	Ⓒ SN 671 841
Refreshments	None	Ⓓ SN 677 836
Ordnance Survey maps	Landranger 135 (Aberystwyth & Machynlleth), Explorer 213 (Aberystwyth & Cwm Rheidol)	Ⓔ SN 693 831

The rumpled hills of Trefeurig were once famous for their silver, lead and copper mines which were worked from prehistoric times until the end of the 20th century. This walk visits some of the scattered mining villages that remain as a legacy of these industrial times – Cwmsymlog, Pen-bont Rhydybeddau and Cwmsebon. The route undulates quite a lot, bringing new vistas every step of the way.

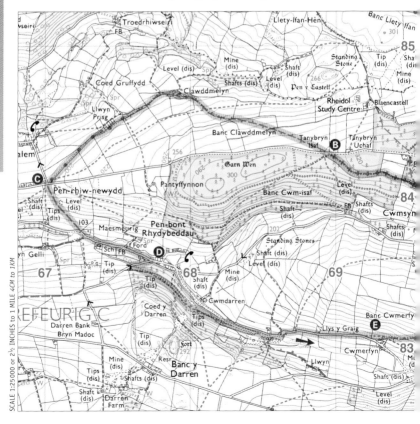

There are a couple of parking areas near Llyn Pendam, and from here walk along the road towards Penrhyn-coch, but, once around the end of the lake, leave the road by branching left onto a wide track. This soon starts to snake downwards into upper Cwmsymlog, passing a clear felled area and providing a stunning view down the length of the valley. When the descending track reaches a junction, keep forward taking the middle option, and heading down towards the chimney of the Cwmsymlog mine **Ⓐ**.

The mine was rich in lead and silver and worked since ancient times. German miners were brought here during the time of Elizabeth I, and the mine seems to have been most productive by about 1620, yielding a profit to the owner of more than £24,000 a year. Later, Cornish steam engines were introduced but this failed to prevent the mine from closing in the 1840s; a brief re-opening, between 1850 and 1880, heralded official closure in 1901.

Walk towards the chimney, but just before reaching it bear sharply right along another track, and follow this the short distance to a signposted bridleway on the left. Leave the track here, through a gate, and onto an ascending grassy track that soon runs along the edge of a plantation, a good place to keep an eye open for crossbills. Rising steadily with improving views down the valley to the coast, the track reaches a gate beyond which it climbs to intercept a wide forest trail. Turn left and follow it out to meet the Penrhyn-coch road **Ⓑ**.

Cross the road to a metal gate and through this bear obliquely left down a large hill pasture. There is no path on the ground, so begin by heading for the left-hand edge of the distant hill with a wind farm on it, then modify the descent to reach a dilapidated fence and locate a fencepost with a waymark on it. From this continue in the same direction, now targeting the rooftops of the farm at Clawddmelyn, and go down to the bottom left-hand corner of the pasture where a gate gives into another sloping pasture. From the gate a discernible broad track descends towards the farm, which is finally

Cwmsymlog mine, Trefeurig

reached through more gates. Walk out along the farm access, emerging in due course at the Penrhyn-coch road once more **C**.

Cross the road and the stile opposite which begins a bridleway. This promptly starts to descend as a broad grassy track, and leading down to the road at Pen-bont Rhydybeddau. Turn left, and walk along the road, passing the village school. Continue as far as the first turning on the right (at a house called Craigffyn), and there **D** turn sharply right onto a narrow, steeply rising lane. Climb as far as a signposted path on the left, and here leave the road. Beyond a gate, a path continues through scrub. When the path forks indistinctly, branch right, climbing onto a higher path that leads up into the edge of woodland before reaching a broad track above the site of the Cwm Darren Mine. The mine, particularly rich in silver, is one of the oldest in the valley,

and has been worked since prehistoric times.

The track soon descends and runs out to meet the valley road. There, turn right, and follow the road for ½ mile (800m), as far as a signposted bridleway on the left (ignore an earlier footpath sign) **E**. Here, leave the road by passing through a gate and onto a rising track. This climbs quite steeply to a gate, beyond which it continues the ascent above the valley, providing stunning views up and down dale. Gradually, the grassy track swings round to climb to a bridlegate and stile. Beyond, it joins a stony track. Go forward onto this, still climbing, but soon crossing a shoulder into the head of Cwmsymlog.

The track presses on around the head of the valley, to and beyond a gate, after which it ambles along easily to another gate giving into a plantation, from which it shortly emerges onto a road near the embanked Llyn Pendam. Turn left to complete the walk. ●

Tresaith and Aberporth

		GPS waypoints
Start	Tresaith	 SN 278 512
Distance	6½ miles (10.4km)	Ⓐ SN 262 516
Approximate time	3½ hours	Ⓑ SN 252 509
Parking	Tresaith (nominal charge)	Ⓒ SN 254 502
Refreshments	Tresaith and Aberporth	Ⓓ SN 263 498
Ordnance Survey maps	Landranger 145 (Cardigan & Mynydd Preseli), Explorer 198 (Cardigan & New Quay)	Ⓔ SN 271 505
		Ⓕ SN 280 509

The tranquillity of the two small beaches around which the village of Tresaith and the larger Aberporth have developed belies the hustle and bustle of the herring industry that once flourished along the coast. Between the two, the Coastal Path makes an agreeable connection before sending the walk into the farmlands inland. This is a quiet ambling route that needs walking, before some of the rights of way seize up altogether.

Leave the car park, turn right and take the road on the left going down to the beach. Walk along the edge of the beach to locate the Coastal Path climbing steps onto the headland, and then continuing between hedgerows, and later running along the edge of a caravan site.

Keep on along the path, and, just before the last houses overlooking the coast, turn left onto a surfaced pathway Ⓐ, and at its end bear right and follow a lane to a road. Turn left and walk up to a road junction, there turning right and passing Gardd Dyffryn Gardens. Walk down the road (Y Ffordd Newydd) that later swings to the right and descends to overlook the beach. Follow the road as it climbs briefly, and then leave it by going forward past the Leaping Dolphin.

Go through a dip where the road crosses the in-flowing stream and climb on the other side, following the road as it bends left. When the road bends right,

climbing steeply, leave it by branching left into Cein Erw and walk down to a wooden gate at the entrance to Ffynnon Gilfach. Go along the path around the edge of houses and onto a footpath, climbing beside a stream to meet the end of a lane where the ongoing path

The Leaping Dolphin, Aberporth

goes forward and around the gable of a house. Now pass along the edge of woodland to a kissing-gate. Through the gate turn left along a field edge, to reach a signpost near a small disused quarry. Here, turn left to a gate, going back into woodland. Climb to a narrow gate at the top edge of the woodland, and then go up the left-hand edge of a field to meet a road **B**. Turn left.

At a T-junction (with the B4333), turn right and after about 110 yds (100m), leave the road by turning left onto a signposted footpath between houses, and going down steps to a stile.

Over the stile go forward across a field to a stile giving onto light woodland. Bear right, and follow the path into the edge of an elongated pasture. Turn left into this (now pathless) and, with the pasture becoming narrower, head down along an old track. Just after a metal gate on the right, cross a waymarked stile beyond which the path descends across a wooded slope to reach a footbridge and stile. From here, climb up the left-hand edge of a scrubby pasture, the path leading to steps and up to a road **C**. Turn right.

After about 110 yds (100m), leave the road by turning left through a bridlegate onto a bridleway leading towards Penlan Farm. The track skirts the farm, and ends just after it turns right to a gate. Through the gate, go left across the end of a green lane, and pass through another gate giving into a large pasture, with the extended garden of the farm on the left. In the pasture, keep left around the field edge to the second metal gate. Turn through this and keep forward along the right-hand edge of another pasture to a gate giving onto a farm track that comes out to meet a lane. Turn right, but after about 220 yds (200m), take the first turning on the left, a sign-posted footpath, along a surfaced lane.

Continue past the farm at Hendre, to follow the lane, now no longer surfaced. The lane comes down to a metal gate at the top end of a rough track **D**. Turn through the gate and go down the track which leads out to meet a road. Turn left and follow the lane up to a T-junction with the B4333, and there go right and, *taking care against approaching traffic*, follow the road for about 440 yds (400m) to a signposted footpath on the left, just before a row of cottages **E**. Leave the road here, going along a rough track at the end of which enter a meadow and keep forward along the left-hand edge which leads to a narrow metal gate. Cross a footbridge and enter the corner of a field. Keep right to the next corner and a stile. Maintain the same direction in the next field, and from the next stile, where the accompanying hedgerow ends. Cross a field to a gate. Beyond this the hedgerow re-appears. Go into the next field at a corner gate and continue alongside the

hedgerow across two fields, and on the far side of the second field keep forward through a gate onto a track enclosed between hedgerows. At the end of the track bear right into a pasture, turning left to go down to a stile near farm buildings.

Over the stile go down a path to meet a track **F**. Follow this to the right, towards a group of buildings, and turn sharply to the left. Having turned left immediately turn through a metal gate onto another hedgerow-enclosed path which goes down into woodland. Follow this down, bearing right at a waymark to meet a lower track, and then, on doing so, turning left. Follow the path as it zigzags down to cross a stream and then climb to a stile, over which bear right up a field edge to another stile in a corner giving onto a road. Turn left and follow the road back to the start. ●

Along the Coastal Path above Aberporth

Borth

		GPS waypoints	
Start	Borth		
Distance	6½ miles (10.5km)	📝 SN 608 890	
Approximate time	3 hours	Ⓐ SN 591 858	
		Ⓑ SN 600 859	
Parking	Borth	Ⓒ SN 612 869	
Refreshments	Borth	Ⓓ SN 616 879	
Ordnance Survey maps	Landranger 135 (Aberystwyth & Machynlleth), Explorer 213 (Aberystwyth & Cwm Rheidol)		

A scenically spectacular switchback of a ride leads south from the coastal village of Borth to a deep-cut glen, where the route turns inland to follow narrow and quiet farm roads back to Borth. Anyone wanting to forgo this inland return can simply elect to retrace the outward route from Wallog, which would give a round trip of five miles (8km) with a lot of up and down – and every step a pleasure to walk. The seaward views are invigorating and offer the chance of spotting an Atlantic grey seal or passing bottle-nosed dolphin.

📝 Borth is a lovely and unpretentious seaside resort built on a shingle spit, and from it head south (towards the conspicuous memorial on a hill) along the seafront, soon branching right into Cliff Road. When the road surfacing ends, move to the right of a garden and onto a rising path, passing through a gate, and soon reaching the war memorial above the sea cliffs of Craig yr Wylfa. This is a lovely viewpoint taking in the great sweep of the bay and farther north into Gwynedd and around the long arm of the Lleyn Peninsula.

From the memorial descend steeply beside a fence to reach the beach at a small cove. Continue on the other side, on a path signposted to Clarach that climbs in zigzags back onto the headland (ignore a stile) finishing with a flurry of steps to gain a dclightful and gentle ascent above the sea cliffs. *There is a risk of collapse in a few spots along the cliff top, so, keep closer to the nearby fence than to the cliff edge.*

The cliffs are impressive and prove to be a wonderful habitat for wild flowers that flourish in the coastal climate – thrift, sea campion, rock samphire, sheep's bit, gorse, harebell, tormentil – and these in turn provide nourishment for butterflies such as common blue, wall brown, small tortoiseshell and small skipper. Down below, cormorants and shags pose on water's-edge rocks while buzzards circle overhead and lesser birds, like linnet, stonechat, goldfinch and meadow pipit, keep a wary eye open for passing peregrine falcons.

The clifftop path undulates a few times providing roller-coaster fun at a sedate pace, and at times very close to the cliff edge. Eventually it descends to a

SCALE 1:25000 or 2½ INCHES to 1 MILE 4CM to 1KM

| 0 | 200 | 400 | 600 | 800 METRES | 1 |
| | 200 | 400 | 600 YARDS | ½ | KILOMETRES MILES |

more substantial incursion at Wallog **A**, where a large house and buildings shelter. Cross an in-flowing stream by a stone footbridge and turn left on the

other side to a gate, beyond which an access lane leads away from the shore.

The lane leads up past Rhoscellan Fawr Farm, and runs out to meet a B-road. Turn left, and, *taking care against approaching traffic*, follow the road for 550 yds (500m) and then branch right

Approaching Wallog

onto a side lane **B** flanked by mature hedgerows that contain blackthorn, hawthorn and honeysuckle.

Follow the lane as far as the turning to Ffosygrafel-uchaf Farm, and here head down towards the farm. Bear right through the farmyard to a gate giving onto a dirt track climbing between hedgerows at the back of the farmhouse. When this turns right into a field, leave it by going forward continuing the original direction, but now following a lovely grassy track with a carpet of scentless mayweed underfoot.

After a short climb, the gradient eases as the track reaches a junction beside gates **C**. Here, take the turning on the right into a field, and go forward with a hedgebank on the left, following this to a field corner. Take the left-hand one of two metal gates, and from it walk forward along the edge of two fields. In the far corner of the second field, a stile gives onto a narrow lane.

From the stile, turn right to a road junction. Go left, following the road north for 770 yds (700m) to another junction **D**, and there turn left again. This road now leads all the way back to the edge of Borth, emerging suddenly at a busy road. Turn right and walk down to the seafront to conclude the walk. ●

Llyn Brianne

Llyn Brianne

		GPS waypoints
Start	Llyn Brianne dam	📷 SN 793 485
Distance	7 miles (11.2km)	Ⓐ SN 788 471
Approximate time	4 hours	Ⓑ SN 783 464
Parking	Llyn Brianne dam	Ⓒ SN 772 479
Refreshments	None	
Ordnance Survey maps	Landranger 147 (Elan Valley & Builth Wells), Explorer 187 (Llandovery)	

The countryside around Llyn Brianne now provides drinking water for South Wales, but there was a time when it sheltered a notorious thief-cum-do-gooder, Twm Siôn Catti. Heavily wooded now, the folded landscape is both austere and attractive, and the reservoir far less of an intrusion than might be imagined. The walk, which spends half of its time on roads, takes the opportunity to visit the RSPB reserve at Dinas, with an optional extension, quite strenuous, to visit the cave of Twm Siôn Catti. The return, from the southern end of the Afon Doethie, is a simple climb into cool woodland and an easy stroll along the reservoir.

Much of the countryside passed through on this walk was criss-crossed by old drove routes, the highways by which cattle, pigs, sheep, turkeys and geese were walked to market. To reduce wear and tear on their feet, the cattle were often shod, rather like a horse, while the turkeys and geese would have their feet dipped in tar to harden them in readiness for the walk.

One of the most famous drovers was Twm Siôn Catti, the illegitimate son of Catherine Jones of Tregaron, but widely believed to have been fathered by Sir John Wynne, lord of the North Wales Gwydir family. Other versions of his parentage claim that his father was a Tregaron man, Dafydd ap Madog ap Hywel Moetheu. Twm was a renowned person, mentioned by poets and writers during his own lifetime. He was born in 1530, married late in life and became a

justice of the peace and later Mayor of Brecon. But legends surround his roguish activities, which may have been a rebellion against the Catholicism prevalent during the reign of Queen Mary. When Elizabeth came to the throne he received an official pardon although the nature of his crimes was not mentioned. To be fair, most of the tales about Twm were the product of the imagination of Llewelyn Pritchard, a 19th-century writer, who wrote *The Adventures and Vagaries of Twm Shon Catti*, which cast him as a popular hero. Twm died in 1609.

📷 From the car park adjoining the dam at Llyn Brianne, walk back out along the access lane to a junction and there turn right along the valley road.

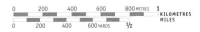

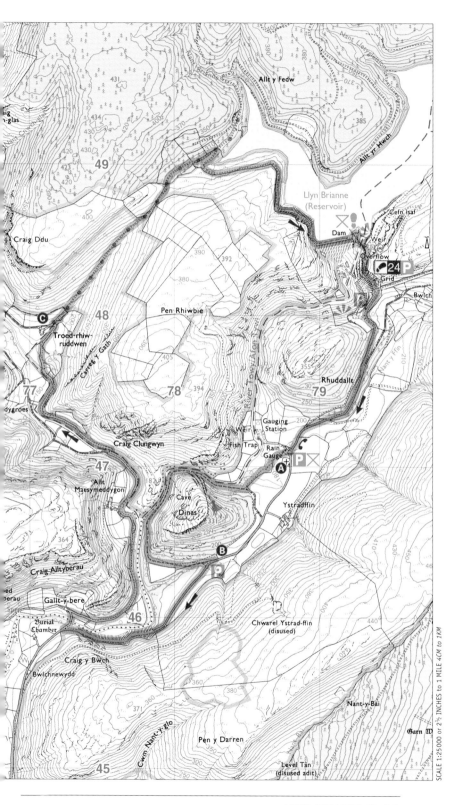

SCALE 1:25000 or 2½ INCHES to 1 MILE 4CM to 1KM

Follow this for about ½ mile (800m) to enter the RSPB Dinas Reserve **Ⓐ**. Buzzards are abundant in this area, while the red kite, for which Wales is famous, are much fewer in number, but still around. Keep an eye open, too, for visiting peregrines, kestrels and merlin.

Cross the car park and go through a kissing-gate and continue along a boardwalk through mixed woodland. When the boardwalk forks, branch right onto a nature trail that follows the course of the Afon Tywi and passes the route up to Twm Siôn Catti's cave. (*This optional extension is strenuous, difficult when wet and leads to a low cave, partially collapsed and needing an 'on-all-fours' approach to enter.*)

When the woodland path forks, branch right to a gate **Ⓑ** and beyond it turn right onto a surfaced lane for another ½ mile (800m), there branching right, crossing the river and turning onto a single track road that leads to the farm at Troed-rhiw-ruddwen. The road surfacing ends at the farm **Ⓒ** from where a rough track heads right, climbing a steep-sided valley.

The track climbs steadily alongside a fence for ½ mile (800m), and then descends briefly to a metal gate giving into a plantation of blue spruce and larch. A good track runs through the plantation to meet a very wide service track around the edge of Llyn Brianne. Turn right onto this and follow a delightful route to and across the dam of the reservoir to return to the start. ●

Llyn Brianne

Pen y Garn

		GPS waypoints	
Start	The Arch on the B4574	🥾	SN 766 756
Distance	7 miles (11.2km)	**Ⓐ**	SN 775 764
Approximate time	3–4 hours	**Ⓑ**	SN 786 772
Parking	The Arch	**Ⓒ**	SN 801 777
Refreshments	Devil's Bridge	**Ⓓ**	SN 787 757
Ordnance Survey maps	Landranger 135 (Aberystwyth & Machynlleth), Explorer 213 (Aberystwyth & Cwm Rheidol)	**Ⓔ**	SN 780 754

Simple of execution, simple of design, this oddly triangular walk climbs to over 2000ft (610m) and provides a stunning and far-reaching view in all directions. Not everyone enjoys walking through a large plantation, but here there is no sense of oppressiveness; large areas of the forest have been cleared, allowing distant views, especially south across the Ystwyth Valley. The way up follows a clear forest trail, the way down likewise, while between the two ends there is a delightful link passing an experimental farm that dates from the early 19th century.

The Arch, built to commemorate the Jubilee of George III in 1810, was constructed by Thomas Johnes of Hafod, who was famous for his pioneering work in upland forest management and landscape design. He is recognised historically as the most visionary, successful and ambitious creator of forests in Wales. He also introduced innovative farming systems to his tenants.

🥾 From the car park set off along the higher of two forest trails, and when shortly confronted by three possible routes, take the middle one climbing gently into the forest. The track soon climbs through an open area and already provides views across to distant hills. The track is flanked by heather, gorse and rosebay willowherb and errant Christmas trees that have wild-seeded from the plantation above.

At the next clearing, with a large hill shoulder of clear-felled land on the right, the main forest trail meets a cross-path at Coed y Ceuleth **Ⓐ**. Keep forward on the main trail, still rising gently, but with ever-improving views south across the Ystwyth Valley. Shortly after the cross-path the forest trail swings right to pass the cleared lump of Truman and brings into view, away to the right, the walk objective, Pen y Garn.

Just after Truman ignore a branching track on the left, and keep forward and then, when the track next forks, branch left always following the main trail through the forest.

At the next track junction **Ⓑ**, keep left now going back among mature pine. Eventually, the track climbs to a view-point overlooking the Nant Rhuddnant,

SCALE 1:25000 or 2½ INCHES to 1 MILE 4CM to 1KM

0	200	400	600	800 METRES	1
0	200	400	600 YARDS	½	

KILOMETRES
MILES

and from here starts to descend and then levels as it runs around the northern shoulder of Pen y Garn. After a short climb ignore a branching track on the right, and continue for a farther 220 yds (200m) to a wide track on the right which doubles back to a gate **C**, and passing below the first of a rash of wind turbines that have been erected here since the first edition of this book.

Follow the ongoing track from which there is a retrospective view to Plynlimon and the Arans beyond. The view south reaches as far as the Brecon Beacons, including Carmarthen Fan and even the summits of Pen y Fan and Corn Du.

Eventually, the climbing eases as the summit of Pen y Garn comes into view on the right. Keep on to a metal gate,

and just after this cross a step-stile on the right and climb beside a fence to another stile at the top giving onto a wide track close by the summit. Cross stiles to reach the summit, which is crowned by a large shelter, and then head down the track, resuming the original direction. The higher and lower tracks meet near another gate. Through this a clear, gated track winds downhill in a series of wide zigzags before heading in a straight line back towards the main forest area.

Just on reaching the forest, the track forks **D**. Bear right to a gate to re-enter the forest. Follow the forest trail as it swings round and crosses a waymarked footpath, which is the lower end of the footpath crossed earlier in the walk at Coed y Ceuleth. Keep forward past this, eventually passing an area on the right of relatively young trees and these end

leading to Gelmast Farm. The farm was originally part of the lands that comprised Strata Florida's Cymystwyth Grange, and eventually passed through marriage to the Johnes family. Gelmast was originally known as 'New Farm' and was built about 1803, and is today one of the very few surviving substantial structures which can be attributed to Thomas Johnes. It was described as an experimental farm and designed as a showcase for Johnes' ideas on grassland management, stocking and dairying. Despite the agricultural purpose of New Farm it was not always occupied by the tenant and his family. During the 19th century, lead miners and their families also lived here as the demands of the expanding metal mining industry attracted an outside workforce to the Cymystwyth area.

Turn into the farmyard and bear left to pass through a gap between buildings. Keep on to a rising track that climbs steadily to a gate at the edge of the forest. Keep forward on a trail between mature and immature plantings. Before long the track rises to the three-way junction encountered at the start of the walk. Turn left here to return to the car park at The Arch. ●

where another footpath crosses the main trail **E**. Here turn right, walking alongside mature trees and now on a narrow path which runs on to meet a footbridge and another wide forest trail beyond. Turn left.

Shortly, turn right on an access track

The Arch

Nant-y-moch

		GPS waypoints
Start	Nant-y-moch Dam	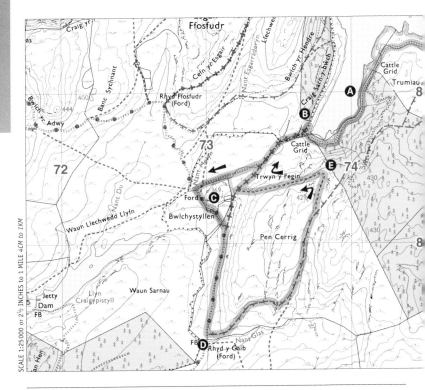 SN 756 862
Distance	7 miles (11.2km)	**A** SN 741 870
Approximate time	3–4 hours	**B** SN 737 867
Parking	At the dam	**C** SN 730 863
Refreshments	Ponterwyd	**D** SN 730 854
Ordnance Survey maps	Landranger 135 (Aberyswyth & Machynlleth), Explorer 213 (Aberystwyth & Cwm Rheidol)	**E** SN 738 865

There are numerous lakes dotted around the Plynlimon massif, but by far the largest is man-made, the Nant-y-moch Reservoir, its arms embracing the isolated mountain, Drosgl. This curious route visits the reservoir, and is very much a walk of two halves: one half simply follows the road (from Ponterwyd to Tal-y-Bont which crosses the reservoir dam and effectively opens up a vast wilderness); the other half takes a quick dip into that wilderness where once lead mining was the principal industry and the derelict cottages that dot the landscape were all occupied.

By driving to point **A** on the map, a roadside lay-by where a forest trail branches left, the whole walk can be shortened by three miles (4.8km), but while driving provides just the same scenery, it misses so much of the unique atmosphere of a place that, until quite recently, was completely treeless. The road up from Ponterwyd crosses the Nant Ceiro. It was near here, at Aber Ceiro Fach, that John Rhys was born in 1840, a man knighted in later life and who became the first professor of Celtic Studies at Oxford University.

Near the dam wall stands a memorial commemorating the victory of Owain Glyndwr at Hyddgen in 1401 – Hyddgen being the river that flows into

Nant-y-moch Dam and Reservoir

the north-eastern arm of the reservoir. From the car park, cross the dam and simply follow the road around the large headland of Trumiau Camddwrmawr to reach the southern end of the western arm of the reservoir **B**. Here, just after a cattle-grid, branch left onto a stony track.

Beyond a gate the track continues into remote countryside with mountains, low, but mountains nonetheless, rising on all sides. There is a tremendous feeling of isolation here, and a simple beauty that comes from a landscape no longer affected by man's attentions.

Continue to follow the track past a small hillock **C** surrounded by the remains of a fence, and when it meets another with Llyn Craigpistyll directly ahead, turn left, soon reaching the ruins of Bwlchystyllen.

Keep following the ongoing track almost as far as a gate and footbridge spanning the Nant Glas at Rhyd y Gaib **D**. Just before the gate, branch left onto another track roughly following the course of the Nant Glas. The track rises steadily onto moorland, bleak and very remote. When it forks, bear right to find that it now climbs steadily, eventually with a plantation coming into view. Just as the high point of the track is reached it seems to fizzle out. In fact, it heads through the

plantation but instantly becomes embroiled in deep mud that makes the old route, technically a motorable road, impassable, even on foot.

So, instead of heading for the plantation, keep forward on a grassy path that rounds the northern end of Pen Carrig just as Nant-y-moch Reservoir comes back into view. Suddenly, there is a dramatic viewpoint **E** as the path rounds a shoulder. Down below is the road where the track first left it, and a step-stile nearby. But there is no right of way in that direction. Instead, turn left across the hill slope and heading on a narrow path that aims for the small hillock **C** rounded earlier in the walk. At times the path is little more than a sheep track and is easily lost, at other times it is pure optimism, but it does lead to the low hillock. There, at the dilapidated fence, it turns right (now trackless) and descends beside a low, moss-covered wall to reach the lower track. Turn right and follow this out to the road. There turn right, and retrace the outward route back to the dam and car park.

●

Looking down on Nant-y-moch

New Quay

		GPS waypoints
Start	New Quay	🖎 SN 387 599
Distance	7½ miles (12km)	Ⓐ SN 380 602
Approximate time	4 hours	Ⓑ SN 364 583
Parking	Near Coastguard Station on Church Road	Ⓒ SN 366 577
Refreshments	New Quay, and pub at Cross Inn	Ⓓ SN 374 568
Ordnance Survey maps	Landranger 145 (Cardigan & Mynydd Preseli), Explorer 198 (Cardigan & New Quay)	Ⓔ SN 384 564
		Ⓕ SN 386 581
		Ⓖ SN 391 591

Anyone walking all the routes described in this book will cover most of Ceredigion's 60-mile coastline, or at least the best parts of it. But in doing so, they will also have discovered some outstanding inland countryside, from wooded glens and babbling streams to quiet country lanes and farmlands patrolled by buzzards, ravens and the occasional red kite. This walk is no exception: the outrun to Cwm Soden is magnificent and marches high above sea cliffs. As the Afon Soden slips almost apologetically into the sea, the route turns inland into the wooded upper glen and a short section of route shared with Walk 5, which will present strong walkers with a longer day, if they want one. Some road walking and a lovely green lane take the walk back into New Quay.

New Quay is one of the oldest ports in Ceredigion, or Cardiganshire as it was, its harbour, embraced between headlands, providing a safe anchorage for boats. Henry Tudor is said to have rested in New Quay on his way to the Battle of Bosworth Field in 1485 which, after victory over Richard III, was to put him on the throne of England. There is a tale that within a year of the visit by the king-to-be, the daughter of the household in which he stayed gave birth to a child, whom they called Harry or Parry. For many years afterwards, anyone who bore the name Parry in this part of Wales is said to claim kinship with the first Welsh king of England.

🖎 Begin the walk from the car park on Church Road, near the Coastguard Station, and turn right out of the car park to a junction with Church Street and Hill Street, but go immediately left into Mason's Square. Follow the road round into Water Street, and shortly turn left into Lewis Terrace. The terrace climbs past houses, and, at the last house, move to the right onto a path rising steeply onto the headland of Penycastell, where the gradient eases and an enclosed path continues, flanked by a wall on the left and bracken and gorse on the other.

The sea cliff path continues above Craig yr Adar (Birds Rock) and is a reminder to keep an eye open seaward for passing birds like fulmar, kittiwake, cormorant, shag and guillemot. Follow the path to a stile after which it crosses into a sloping coastal pasture to another stile with the cliffs of Penmoelciliau rising in the distance. After a third stile the path begins to descend a little as it rounds a small bay **A**, and then goes down more steeply, providing improving views of the cliffs farther south. Descend steeply into a narrow ravine from which the path escapes up steps and then along a path to a signpost. Turn right here for Cwmtydu.

Another down and up to complete rounding the small bay leads to another stile shortly after which turn right through a hedge gap and walk down to a footbridge. Beyond, the path climbs steadily once more, turning right through a gate at the top of the climb to resume the Coastal Path above the steep sea slopes of Coybal. A gate overlooks another small bay, which marks the turning point of the walk. Head down to the bay, and turn inland on a lovely path that rises gradually and later heads into woodland. This is Cwm Soden, a tranquil and delightful place to be **B**.

The path reaches a sign at the edge of the National Trust Byrlip Estate. Here, turn right to a footbridge, crossing this and immediately turning left on a signposted path for Nanternis **C**. [*By turning right immediately after the*

The cliffs above New Quay

footbridge, walkers will link in with Walk 5 for a trek across to Cwmtydu. This will add 3 miles (4.8km) to this walk.]

A stony path climbs to a clearing with a stand of aspen trees on the left.

Folklore has it that the aspen was the tree used to make the cross on which Christ was crucified, and that thereafter, as a mark of shame, the tree has trembled in fear. It is true that the aspen is very distinctive because of its

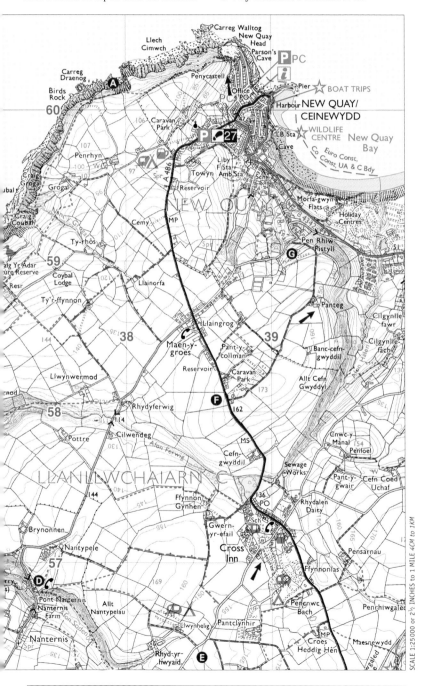

SCALE 1:25000 or 2½ INCHES to 1 MILE 4CM to 1KM

Heading down Cwm Soden

shimmering leaves, which have dark upper sides and white underneath, something eastern authorities say signifies yin and yang.

Across the clearing, the path goes back into woodland soon reaching a kissing-gate beyond which it begins a sheltered path embowered by broad-leaved trees. Soon after the path starts to rise, it forks. Branch right at a wooden post and continue at an easier gradient. The path leads down to a stile giving onto a broad access track alongside the Afon Soden. Keep forward along the track to a gate, and follow the ongoing track out to meet a road near a cottage **D**.

Cross the road and turn right onto a signposted path through a metal gate. A grassy path rises alongside a hedgebank to a ruined building. Keep to the right of the ruin and, a short way farther on, leave the track by climbing wooden steps on the left, and a steep gorse slope above, to another stile giving into a large field. Follow the field boundary round to a metal gate. From this bear half-right across the next field to another gate, through which go left along the field boundary to a stile/wall/stile combination in the far corner emerging into another field.

Head down beside a hedge on the right to find a gap on the far side. Turn right through this, continuing as far as a stile on the left giving onto an enclosed path alongside a caravan site. Follow this to a surfaced lane at the entrance to the site, and keep forward to meet a road. Turn left **E**.

Follow the road to Cross Inn, and at the road junction turn left and, *taking great care against approaching traffic*, follow the A-road for about ½ mile (800m), climbing gently. At the top of the climb, just after the first cottage on the right at Maen-y-groes, leave the road by turning right onto a signposted bridleway **F** that heads along an old green lane past another caravan site.

When the track reaches Panteg Farm keep forward on a grassy path between hedgerows. This passes through a gate then descends very agreeably towards unseen New Quay, passing through a sheltered section that proves a fine habitat for hart's tongue and lady-fern and finally emerges onto a minor road **G**. Turn right and follow the road left. As the road bends right at the White House, keep forward on a path descending alongside houses to a kissing-gate beyond which it becomes enclosed by hedgerows.

The path emerges at a house called Glyngoleu. Follow the path past the house, turn into a narrow lane, and turn right. At a minor road junction, keep left, descending between houses and at the back of a school to a road junction. Turn into Margaret Street. Walk up past a turning to the beach, and take the next turning right (Park Street). Follow this round as it becomes Hill Street, and finally ends at the bottom of Church Road near the start. ●

Teifi Pools Walk

Start	Strata Florida	GPS waypoints
Distance	9 miles (14.5km)	🖉 SN 746 657
Approximate time	4–5 hours	Ⓐ SN 791 665
Parking	Strata Florida	Ⓑ SN 786 682
Refreshments	Pontrhydfendigaid	Ⓒ SN 766 667
Ordnance Survey maps	Landranger 135 (Aberystwyth & Machynlleth), Explorer 187 (Llandovery) and [small amount on] 213 (Aberystwyth & Cwm Rheidol)	Ⓓ SN 766 656

'A Walk on the Wild Side' might be an apt title for this excursion, although it has been rather tamed by the availability for some time of a reservoir access road that makes the circuit of the 'pools' so much easier. But wilderness there is, and the walk should not be underestimated, wandering as it does through rugged, hummocky terrain and seeming to be constantly changing direction. There is a splendid sense of isolation here and a pleasure that comes from exploring with red kites for company.

🖉 Starting from Strata Florida, the route makes the most of the walk in (and out) through a lovely green valley, but by parking at a small lay-by near Tyncwm Farm nearly three miles (4.5km) can be lopped off the total distance.

It begins down the lane near Strata Florida and simply follows it to Tyncwm Farm. There, opposite a disused chapel with some lovely lichenous growths on its walls, the route turns left to pass through the farm (waymarked) and then onto a steadily rising grassy path through the Nant Egnant. The track climbs easily for a while before easing. As it runs on to cross the valley stream go through a gate beyond which the track continues into open country. A long steady pull leads to a large cairn beyond which the gradient eases, shortly after which the first pool,

Ascending on the Teifi Pools Walk

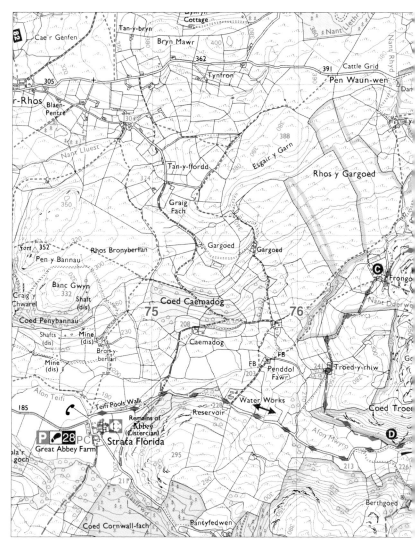

Llyn Egnant, comes into view **A**.

Through a gate the track continues to the west of the lake, where the ongoing track is now surfaced. Beyond the end of Llyn Egnant the track climbs briefly and then continues into a large moorland expanse where it meets another track. The landscape here is austere, barren, convoluted and rocky, but there was a time, before the sheep-farming Cistercian monks came on the scene, when all of this would have been wooded.

Turn left and follow the road as far

as a signboard overlooking the northern end of Llyn Teifi, where the track forks **B**. Branch left and head for the dam of Llyn Teifi, passing through a gate. At the road end, keep to the right of a fence at the end of which bear right on a grassy path passing round the end of a rocky outcrop, and soon swinging left to go down to a stile and a stream. Bear right on an indistinct grassy path at first roughly parallel with a fence on the right and then maintaining a mild flirtation with the infant River Teifi.

The ongoing path picks a way across

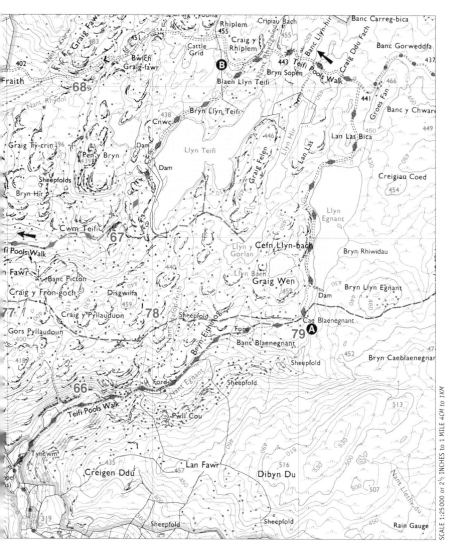

SCALE 1:25000 or 2½ INCHES to 1 MILE 4CM to 1KM

a stretch of marshy ground, across which it is waymarked, and then starts to climb a little to round a hill shoulder, improving as it goes into a hill track. Gradually, the track swings round to Frongoch Farm **C**. Cross a step-stile and go between farm buildings to locate a waymarked ladder stile giving onto a vehicle track that passes through a gate and ascends gently to enter a large hill pasture near a quarry. Bear right alongside a low wall topped by a fence, soon with the church and abbey at Strata Florida coming into view.

The track now descends to Troed-y-rhiw Farm. Just on passing the farm, go left over a step-stile onto a broad grassy path which, shortly after crossing another stile, swings around as a narrow path across the steep slope of a hill shoulder and then continues through bracken and on to meet the road **D**.

Those who have started at Tyncwm, turn left. Those heading back to Strata Florida, turn right. ●

Further Information

The National Trust

Anyone who likes visiting places of natural beauty and/or historic interest has cause to be grateful to the National Trust. Without it, many such places would probably have vanished by now.

It was in response to the pressures on the countryside posed by the relentless march of Victorian industrialisation that the trust was set up in 1895. Its founders, inspired by the common goals of protecting and conserving Britain's national heritage and widening public access to it, were Sir Robert Hunter, Octavia Hill and Canon Rawnsley: respectively a solicitor, a social reformer and a clergyman. The latter was particularly influential. As a canon of Carlisle Cathedral and vicar of Crosthwaite (near Keswick), he was concerned about threats to the Lake District and had already been active in protecting footpaths and promoting public access to open countryside. After the flooding of Thirlmere in 1879 to create a large reservoir, he became increasingly convinced that the only effective way to guarantee protection was outright ownership of land.

The purpose of the National Trust is to preserve areas of natural beauty and sites of historic interest by acquisition, holding them in trust for the nation and making them available for public access and enjoyment. Some of its properties have been acquired through purchase, but many have been donated. Nowadays it is not only one of the biggest landowners in the country, but also one of the most active conservation charities, protecting 581,113 acres (253,176 ha) of land, including 555 miles (892km) of coastline, and more than 300 historic properties in England, Wales and Northern Ireland. (There is a separate National Trust for Scotland, which was set up in 1931.)

Furthermore, once a piece of land has come under National Trust ownership, it is difficult for its status to be altered. As a result of parliamentary legislation in 1907, the Trust was given the right to declare its property inalienable, so ensuring that in any subsequent dispute it can appeal directly to parliament.

As it works towards its dual aims of conserving areas of attractive countryside and encouraging greater public access (not easy to reconcile in this age of mass tourism), the Trust provides an excellent service for walkers by creating new concessionary paths and waymarked trails, maintaining stiles and footbridges and combating the ever-increasing problem of footpath erosion.

For details of membership, contact the National Trust at the address on page 95.

The Ramblers' Association

No organisation works more actively to protect and extend the rights and interests of walkers in the countryside than the Ramblers' Association. Its aims are clear: to foster a greater knowledge, love and care of the countryside; to assist in the protection and enhancement of public rights of way and areas of natural beauty; to work for greater public access to the countryside; and to encourage more people to take up rambling as a healthy, recreational leisure activity.

It was founded in 1935 when, following the setting up of a National Council of Ramblers' Federation in 1931, a number of federations in London, Manchester, the Midlands and elsewhere came together to create a more effective pressure group, to deal with such problems as the disappearance or obstruction of footpaths, the prevention of access to open mountain and moorland, and increasing hostility from landowners. This was the era of the mass trespasses, when there were sometimes violent confrontations between ramblers and gamekeepers, especially on the moorlands of the Peak District.

Since then the Ramblers' Association has played a key role in preserving and developing the national footpath network, supporting the creation of national parks and encouraging the designation and waymarking of long-distance routes.

Our freedom of access to the countryside, now enshrined in legislation, is still in its early years and requires constant vigilance. But over and above this there will always be the problem of footpaths being illegally obstructed, disappearing through lack of use, or being extinguished by housing or road construction.

It is to meet such problems and dangers that the Ramblers' Association exists and represents the interests of all walkers. The address to write to for information on the Ramblers' Association and how to become a member is given on page 95.

 Walkers and the Law

The *Countryside and Rights of Way Act 2000 (CRoW)* extends the rights of access previously enjoyed by walkers in England and Wales. Implementation of these rights began on 19 September 2004. The Act amends existing legislation and for the first time provides access on foot to certain types of land – defined as mountain, moor, heath, down and registered common land.

Where You Can Go
Rights of Way
Prior to the introduction of *CRoW* walkers could only legally access the countryside along public rights of way. These are either 'footpaths' (for walkers only) or 'bridleways' (for walkers, riders on horseback and pedal cyclists). A third category called 'Byways open to all traffic' (BOATs), is used by motorised vehicles as well as those using non-mechanised transport. Mainly they are green lanes, farm and estate roads, although occasionally they will be found crossing mountainous area.

Rights of way are marked on Ordnance Survey maps. Look for the green broken lines on the Explorer maps, or the red dashed lines on Landranger maps.

The term 'right of way' means exactly what it says. It gives a right of passage over what, for the most part, is private land. Under pre-CRoW legislation walkers were required to keep to the line of the right of way and not stray onto land on either side. If you did inadvertently wander off the right of way, either because of faulty map reading or because the route was not clearly indicated on the ground, you were technically trespassing.

Local authorities have a legal obligation to ensure that rights of way are kept clear and free of obstruction, and are signposted where they leave metalled roads. The duty of local authorities to install signposts extends to the placing of signs along a path or way, but only where the authority considers it necessary to have a signpost or waymark to assist persons unfamiliar with the locality.

The New Access Rights
Access Land
As well as being able to walk on existing rights of way, under the new legislation you now have access to large areas of open land. You can of course continue to use rights of way footpaths to cross this land, but the main difference is that you can now lawfully leave the path and wander at will, but only in areas designated as access land.

Where to Walk
Areas now covered by the new access rights – Access Land – are shown on Ordnance Survey Explorer maps bearing the access land symbol on the front cover.

'Access Land' is shown on Ordnance Survey maps by a light yellow tint surrounded by a pale orange border. New orange coloured 'i' symbols on the maps will show the location of permanent access information boards installed by the access authorities.

Restrictions
The right to walk on access land may lawfully be restricted by landowners. Landowners can, for any reason, restrict access for up to 28 days in any year. They cannot however close the land:

- on bank holidays;
- for more than four Saturdays and Sundays in a year;
- on any Saturday from 1 June to 11 August; or
- on any Sunday from 1 June to the end of September.

They have to provide local authorities with five working days' notice before the date of closure unless the land involved is an area of less than five hectares or the closure is for less than four hours. In these cases landowners only need to provide two hours' notice.

Whatever restrictions are put into place on access land they have no effect on existing rights of way, and you can continue to walk on them.

Dogs

Dogs can be taken on access land, but must be kept on leads of two metres or less between 1 March and 31 July, and at all times where they are near livestock. In addition landowners may impose a ban on all dogs from fields where lambing takes place for up to six weeks in any year. Dogs may be banned from moorland used for grouse shooting and breeding for up to five years.

In the main, walkers following the routes in this book will continue to follow existing rights of way, but a knowledge and understanding of the law as it affects walkers, plus the ability to distinguish access land marked on the maps, will enable anyone who wishes to depart from paths that cross access land either to take a shortcut, to enjoy a view or to explore.

General Obstructions

Obstructions can sometimes cause a problem on a walk and the most common of these is where the path across a field has been ploughed over. It is legal for a farmer to plough up a path provided that it is restored within two weeks. This does not always happen and you are faced with the dilemma of following the line of the path, even if this means treading on crops, or walking round the edge of the field. Although the latter course of action seems

Glossary of Welsh Words

This list gives some of the more common elements in Welsh place-names, which will allow readers to understand otherwise meaningless words and appreciate the relationship between place-names and landscape features. Place-names often have variant spellings, and the more common of these are given here.

aber	estuary, confluence	llyn	lake
afon	river	maen	stone
bach, fach	small	maes	field
bryn	mound, hill	mawr, fawr	big, large
bwlch	pass	moel, foel	rounded hill
caer	fort	morfa	sea marsh
capel	chapel	mynydd, fynydd	mountain
carn, carnedd	cairn	nant	brook, stream
castell	castle	newydd	new
ceunant	gorge, ravine	pair	cauldron
coed	wood	pen	head, top
craig	crag	pentre(f)	village
crib	narrow ridge	pont, bont	bridge
cwm	cirque, valley	pwll	pool
drws	door, gap (pass)	rhaedr	waterfall
dyffryn	valley	sarn	causeway
eglwys, llan	church	traeth	beach, shore
ffordd	road	tre(f), dre(f)	town
glyn	glen	tŷ, ty	house
llan, eglwys	church	twll	hole
llwybr	path	ynys	island

Countryside Access Charter

Your rights of way are:

- public footpaths – on foot only. Sometimes waymarked in yellow
- bridleways – on foot, horseback and pedal cycle. Sometimes waymarked in blue
- byways (usually old roads), most 'roads used as public paths' and, of course, public roads – all traffic has the right of way

Use maps, signs and waymarks to check rights of way. Ordnance Survey Explorer and Landranger maps show most public rights of way

On rights-of-way you can:

- take a pram, pushchair or wheelchair if practicable
- take a dog (on a lead or under close control)
- take a short route round an illegal obstruction or remove it sufficiently to get past

You have a right to go for recreation to:

- public parks and open spaces – on foot
- most commons near older towns and cities – on foot and sometimes on horseback
- private land where the owner has a formal agreement with the local authority

In addition you can use the following by local or established custom or consent, but ask for advice if you are unsure:

- many areas of open country, such as moorland, fell and coastal areas, especially those in the care of the National Trust, and some commons
- some woods and forests, especially those owned by the Forestry Commission
- country parks and picnic sites
- most beaches
- canal towpaths
- some private paths and tracks Consent sometimes extends to horse-riding and cycling

For your information:

- county councils and London boroughs maintain and record rights-of-way, and register commons
- obstructions, dangerous animals, harassment and misleading signs on rights-of-way are illegal and you should report them to the county council
- paths across fields can be ploughed, but must normally be reinstated within two weeks
- landowners can require you to leave land to which you have no right of access
- motor vehicles are normally permitted only on roads, byways and some 'roads used as public paths'

---

the most sensible, it does mean that you would be trespassing.

Other obstructions can vary from overhanging vegetation to wire fences across the path, locked gates or even a cattle feeder on the path.

Use common sense. If you can get round the obstruction without causing damage, do so. Otherwise only remove as much of the obstruction as is necessary to secure passage.

If the right of way is blocked and cannot be followed, there is a long-standing view that in such circumstances there is a right to deviate, but this cannot wholly be relied on. Although it is accepted in law that highways (and that includes rights of way) are for the public service, and if the usual track is impassable, it is

for the general good that people should be entitled to pass into another line. However, this should not be taken as indicating a right to deviate whenever a way becomes impassable. If in doubt, retreat.

Report obstructions to the local authority and/or the Ramblers' Association.

 ## Global Positioning System (GPS)

What is GPS?

GPS is a worldwide radio navigation system that uses a network of 24 satellites and receivers, usually hand-held, to calculate positions. By measuring the time it takes a signal to reach the receiver, the distance from the satellite can be estimated. Repeat this with several satellites and the receiver can then use triangulation to establish the position of the receiver.

How to use GPS with Ordnance Survey mapping

Each of the walks in this book includes GPS co-ordinate data that reflects the walk position points on Ordnance Survey maps.

GPS and OS maps use different models for the earth and co-ordinate systems, so when you are trying to relate your GPS position to features on the map the two will differ slightly. This is especially the case with height, as the model that relates the GPS global co-ordinate system to height above sea level is very poor.

When using GPS with OS mapping, some distortion – up to 16ft (5m) – will always be present. Moreover, individual features on maps may have been surveyed only to an accuracy of 23ft (7m) (for 1:25000 scale maps), while other features, e.g. boulders, are usually only shown schematically.

In practice, this should not cause undue difficulty, as you will be near enough to your objective to be able to spot it.

How to use the GPS data in this book

There are various ways you can use the GPS data in this book.

1. Follow the route description while checking your position on your receiver when you are approaching a position point.

2. You can also use the positioning information on your receiver to verify where you are on the map.

3. Alternatively, you can use some of the proprietary software that is available. At the simple end there is inexpensive software, which lets you input the walk positions (waypoints), download them to the gps unit and then use them to assist your navigation on the walks.

At the upper end of the market Ordnance Survey maps are available in electronic form. Most come with software that enables you to enter your walking route onto the map, download it to your gps unit and use it, alongside the route description, to follow the route.

 Safety on the Hills

The hills, mountains and moorlands of Britain, though of modest height compared with those in many other countries, need to be treated with respect. Friendly and inviting in good weather, they can quickly be transformed into wet, misty, windswept and potentially danger-ous areas of wilderness in bad weather. Even on an outwardly fine and settled summer day, conditions can rapidly deteriorate. In winter, of course, the weather can be even more erratic and the hours of daylight are much shorter.

It is advisable, therefore, to always take both warm and waterproof clothing, sufficient nourishing food, a hot drink, first-aid kit, torch and whistle. Wear suitable footwear such as strong walking boots or shoes that give a good grip over rocky terrain and on slippery slopes. Try to obtain a local weather forecast and bear it in mind before you start. Do not be afraid to abandon your proposed route and return to your starting point in the event of a sudden and unexpected deterioration in the weather. Do not go alone. Allow enough time to finish the walk well before nightfall.

Most of the walks described in this book do not venture into remote wilderness areas and will be safe to do, given due care and respect, at any time of year in all but the most unreasonable weather. Indeed, a crisp, fine winter day often provides perfect conditions for walking, with firm ground underfoot and a clarity that it is not possible to achieve in the other seasons of the year. A few walks in this book, however, are suitable only for reasonably fit and experienced hill walkers who are able to use a compass, and these routes should definitely not be tackled by anyone else during the winter months or in bad weather, especially high winds and mist. These are indicated in the general description that precedes each of the walks.

Further Information

Useful Organisations

Cadw: Welsh Assembly Government
Plas Carew, Unit 5/7, Cefn Coed,
Parc Nant garw, Cardiff CF15 7QQ
Tel. 01443 336000
www.cadw-wales.gov.uk

Coed Cymru
The Old Sawmill, Tregynon,
Newtown, Powys SY16 3PL
Tel. 01686 650777
www.coedcymru.org.uk

Campaign for the Protection of Rural Wales
Ty Gwyn, 31 High Street, Welshpool,
Powys SY21 7YD
Tel. 01938 552525
www.cprw.org.uk

Countryside Council for Wales
Maes-y-Ffynnon, Penrhosgarnedd,
Bangor, Gwynedd LL57 2DW
Tel. 0845 1306 229
www.ccw.gov.uk

National Trust Office for Wales
Trinity Square, Llandudno LL30 2DE
Tel. 01492 860 123
www.nationaltrust.org.uk

Ordnance Survey
Romsey Road, Maybush, Southampton
SO16 4GU
Tel. 08456 05 05 05
www.ordnancesurvey.co.uk

Ramblers' Association Wales
3 Coopers Yard, Curran Road, Cardiff
CF10 5NB
Tel. +44 (0) 29 2064 4308
www.ramblers.org.uk/wales

Royal Society for the Protection of Birds (RSPB)
The Lodge, Sandy, Beds SG19 2DL
Tel. 01767 680551
www.rspb.org.uk

Tourist Information Centres
Tourist Information Centres are usually
open daily between 10.00 and 17.30. Of those listed below, all except Borth are open all year; Borth is open between Easter and October.

Aberaeron: 01545 570602
Aberystwyth: 01970 612125
Borth: 01970 871174
Cardigan: 01239 613230

Wales Tourist Board
www.visitwales.co.uk

Youth Hostels Association,
Trevelyan House, Dimple Road, Matlock,
Derbyshire DE4 3YH.
Tel. 0870 770 6113
www.yha.org.uk

 Ordnance Survey maps

The walks described in this guide are covered by Ordnance Survey 1:50 000 scale (1¼ inches to 1 mile or 2cm to 1km) Landranger map sheets 125, 135, 136, 137, 138, 146, 147, 148, 149, 160 and 161.

These all-purpose maps are packed with information to help you explore the areas. Viewpoints, picnic sites, places of interest and caravan and camping sites are shown as well as public rights of way information such as footpaths and bridleways.

To examine Ceredigion in more detail and especially if you are planning walks, the Ordnance Survey Explorer maps at 1:25 000 scale (2½ inches to 1 mile or 4cm to 1km) are ideal. Maps covering the area are:

OL23 (Cadair ldris & Llyn Tegid)
187 (Llandovery)
198 (Cardigan & New Quay)
213 (Aberystwyth & Cwm Rheidol)

To get to Ceredigion use the Ordnance Survey Great Britain Routeplanner at 1:625 000 (1 inch to 10 miles or 4cm to 25km) scale or Road Map 6 (Wales and West Midlands) at 1:250 000 scale.

Ordnance Survey maps and guides are available from most booksellers, stationers and newsagents.

www.totalwalking.co.uk

www.totalwalking.co.uk
is the official website of the Jarrold
Pathfinder and Short Walks guides. This
interactive website features a wealth of
information for walkers – from the latest
news on route diversions and advice from
professional walkers to product news, free
sample walks and promotional offers.